Welfare Gains
from
Advertising

Welfare Gains from Advertising

The Problem of Regulation

Dean A. Worcester, Jr.
with Ronald Nesse

American Enterprise Institute for Public Policy Research
Washington, D.C.

Dean A. Worcester, Jr., is professor of economics at the University of Washington.

Ronald J. Nesse is a predoctoral associate in economics at the University of Washington.

Library of Congress Cataloging in Publication Data

Worcester, Dean A.
  Welfare gains from advertising.

  (AEI studies ; 188)
  Includes index.
  1.   Advertising.   2.   Industrial organization (Economic theory).
3. Competition.   4. Welfare economics. I. Nesse, Ronald, joint author.
II.   Title.   III.   Series: American Enterprise Institute
for Public Policy Research.   AEI studies; 188.
HF5833.W67   659.1   78-6625
ISBN 0-8447-3290-7

AEI Studies 188

Printed in the United States of America

CONTENTS

PREFACE

This study advances the idea that the modern analysis of markets, painstakingly developed over four decades to increase its relevance to real problems, may have misdirected economic analysis and provided a persuasive rationale for government policies that take us further away from desired social objectives. Proposals to regulate advertising by private enterprises provides a convenient avenue of approach to this investigation for at least two important reasons.

First, advertising by private firms obviously attempts to influence people in ways that enhance a private interest, often that of a large firm that is believed already to possess a degree of monopoly power. Consequently, advertising is perceived as favoring private monopoly and is for that reason legitimately subject to regulation by a government assumed to be consumer-oriented and therefore dedicated to achieving goals described by the formal theory of competition. Yet advertising may in fact have opposite effects, and its regulation may produce monopoly that otherwise would not exist.

Second, sophisticated econometric analysis has been brought to bear on hypotheses developed from the modern theory of markets. Such analysis often finds statistically significant relationships that confirm the links among advertising intensity, concentration, and profits expected if monopoly exists. Although these relationships are subject to conflicting interpretations even on narrow statistical grounds, they buttress the case for government regulation of business to "improve the quality of competition" in the private sector. This raises the more fundamental subject of this book: the model of competition relevant for judging the quality of competition that is suitable as a guide for regulation.

Present-day conventional analysis is based on an austere model of economic relationships that has proved valuable as an engine of discovery. Its success depends in large part on simple, "clean" concepts that produce hard-edged hypotheses in a sort of intellectual laboratory. It abstracts from all conditions thought to have small importance to the specific matter under investigation. These neglected conditions typically include, among others, the geographical dispersion of suppliers and customers, the time required to respond to changed conditions, and the time and expense involved to learn about opportunities. None of these can safely be neglected when judging the quality of competition or the role that advertising plays in modern markets. Yet they are neglected when, as is typically the case, criteria for "competitive" efficiency are taken directly from modern theory and set up as guides for regulation and public policy.

Used in this way, present-day conventional analysis is biased toward the discovery of inefficiencies, "welfare losses," resulting from private choices by businesspeople and consumers. Such choices are said to fail to ensure technical efficiency of resource use, to provide an inferior assortment and quality of products, not to respond to true consumer preferences, and not to distribute income and wealth appropriately. Government, action, guided by appropriate economic analysis, is advocated by some economists to improve performance in each of these dimensions. This study argues in contrast that deterioration of performance is the more probable outcome of regulation because the model upon which the findings of poor performance rest is inappropriate and because the recommendations for government action rest upon an unacceptable theory of government regulation.

A contest has existed for about a hundred years between those who believe legitimate activity requires government sanction and those who find private actions consonant with the public interest. The regulation of advertising is part of this basically political contest. From this point of view Joseph A. Schumpeter would probably judge the present book a skirmish in a hundred-year-old lost cause. He wrote,

> It is an error to believe that political attack (on private business) arises primarily from grievance and that it can be turned by justification. Political criticism cannot be met effectively by rational argument . . . so capitalism stands its trial before judges who already have the sentence of death in their pockets. They are going to pass it, whatever defense they may hear; the only success victorious defense can possibly produce is a change in the indictment. Utilitarian reason is in any case weak as a prime mover of group action. In no case is it a match for the extra-rational determination of conduct.[1]

---

[1]Joseph A. Schumpeter, *Capitalism, Socialism and Democracy*, 3rd ed. (New York: Harper & Row, 1950), p. 144.

The skirmish, nevertheless, is worth fighting. Schumpeter never claimed to know the future, but only extrapolated trends he discovered.[2] He noted that unforeseen situations can halt or divert such trends. One unforeseen development that may do this is the burgeoning belief in the ineffectiveness and petty, and not so petty, tyranny of government agencies, which are beginning to make business, even very big business, look good by comparison. But this by itself will not suffice; a positive appreciation of the available alternatives and the social benefits from private activities is needed. Some appreciation exists, but it suffers from poor articulation and even more so from excessive reliance on a crude "materialism" that seeks justification in the piling up of goods and services with little apparent regard for shifts that make jobs and occupations obsolete or that move work from one region to another. It also somehow fails to make evident the brute fact that business more than any governmental, political, or other essentially reformist organization is by its nature composed of volunteer agents competing at their own risk to serve the desires of consumers as well as they can determine what they are and how they can be served. This is often as poorly perceived by businesspeople as it is by their critics.

Businesspeople are agents of consumers and serve them without judging them. To be sure, some individual businesspeople refuse to cater to some consumer tastes, but others will serve them well—far too well in the opinion of those who mistrust the judgment of their fellow citizens and condemn those who cater to their "unhealthy" desires. Those sharing majority opinion often energize it with the force of the state so as to impede or deny access to alcohol, heroin, cyclamates, certain children's nightwear, or whatever. It has not always stopped with specific goods. Moralists have used their control of government to deny some people access to their religion, their political party, and the press. In contrast, private business has always catered to diverse needs. In the face of prohibitions, people find ways to satisfy, to a degree, their officially despised desires as well as those that are officially approved. This catholicism gives all business a pragmatic, amoral cast that calls for the opprobrium of some and the suspicion of all who question their neighbors' tastes and especially the potential effect of those tastes upon their children. Yet, by their nature, businesspeople pay humanity the compliment of treating it as if it were composed of individuals who are responsible and able to learn and of colleagues or suppliers who are able to perform and to cooperate effectively. This contrasts rather well with the alternative view of customers and em-

---

[2]Ibid., see p. 416 for, literally, his last word on the subject.

ployees as being so hopelessly ill-informed, impulsive, and gullible as to need perpetual surveillance and protection by their betters.

Businesspeople serve others including those they dislike, because it is in their interest to do so, but few recognize this service and the value it creates. This blindness grants a moral advantage to non-businesspeople who claim a selfless motive, though they may serve most people poorly and may have relatively few successes. This brings us to the skirmish at hand. Perhaps it can improve perceptions.

For reasons just given, commercial speech, advertising, is already more suspect and constrained than literary, journalistic, and political speech. Today's moralists seek new ground for further constraints. The task appears simple, for further restrictions on advertising are said to lower prices to consumers by reducing needless costs and monopolists' profits. Upon examination, neither of these good things is at all likely to be forthcoming. Instead, costs will rise and consumers will suffer. The reasons for these conclusions are the subjects of Chapters 2 and 3. But such findings will not suffice to forestall the counterproductive constraints that are proposed. To quote Schumpeter once more, "Such refutation may tear the rational garb of attack but can never reach the extra-rational driving power that always lurks behind it."[3] It is necessary to examine the alternatives, and to look much more closely at the characteristics of economic theorizing that have obscured vitally important aspects of economic and social life. This is attempted in Chapters 4 and 5.

A substantial debt is owed to several people who read the first draft of this book. John S. McGee's comments and marginal notes were especially helpful. Yoram Barzel's insightful criticism saved me from several errors. I profited from some literature that Stanley I. Ornstein brought to my attention. Judy Cox gave me the benefit of a careful reading, and Levis Kochin deepened the analysis at two points. Douglass C. North raised questions that forced me to clarify and improve several points in the Preface and Chapters 4 and 5. Ronald Nesse did so much, especially with respect to the econometric literature, that he deserves listing on the title page. None has read the final draft, and responsibility for errors of omission and commission fall with undiluted weight on me.

---

[3] Ibid., p. 144.

1

Introduction

Highly sophisticated econometric models uncover statistically significant relationships between advertising, concentration, and profits. Since concentration of a large proportion of an industry's sales or employment in a small number of firms and a higher than average profit are both evidence of monopoly, these findings support and inspire a rising but misplaced enthusiasm for more public regulation of private sector industries that advertise heavily. Improved competition and services to the consumer are supposed to follow more regulation. However, neither the theory underlying the econometric analyses nor the implications of the analyses themselves provide valid support for government regulation of advertising or of the conditions that induce firms to advertise. The first section of this study tries to show why this judgment is correct.

The theoretical base for the econometric studies is the now conventional monopolistic and imperfect competition variations of welfare economics, which have been painstakingly developed for more than four decades. The studies are in a significant sense biased to discover "market failures" when individuals and enterprises are allowed to make their own choices in markets. The base is biased, especially for policy purposes, because it does not subject all important constraints to analysis; for that reason the studies inevitably find a plethora of "externalities" and other inefficiencies. Thus individual choices in markets are thought to fail to ensure technical efficiency of resource use, to produce an inferior assortment and quality of products, not to respond to true consumer preferences, to fall short of full employment, to contribute to inflation, not to conserve resources properly, nor to distribute income or wealth appropriately. If advertising were a cause of monopoly, it would contribute to the first three and the last named of these market failures.

1

Present-day economic theory is hospitable to government activities to correct these shortcomings. Yet government is also composed of individuals who must be organized, informed, and motivated as well as empowered if corrective action is to succeed. These activities inevitably consume valuable resources, and less than perfect performance must be expected. So it is not acceptable simply to suppose that the discovery of a genuine "market failure" in the private sector is tantamount to the discovery of a better use of resources. The loss attributable to the failure may be less than the cost of "corrective" action.

A subtler but fundamental problem intimately related to the greatest strength of economic theory underlies and compounds the difficulties alluded to in the preceding paragraph. Economic theory is a powerful engine of discovery, but it is ill-suited to the role of guiding policy. It yields testable hypotheses based upon rational individual choice subject to the constraints operative at the time. Many hypotheses derived from this theorizing stand up well to empirical investigation. Understanding acquired with the aid of economic theory also yields valid prediction of responses to changed constraints. But the same approach is less well-suited when the problem is to judge the relative quantities of "social welfare" resulting from alternative sets of conditions where some individuals are better off under one set of conditions and worse off under another. The final chapters of this study explore this problem and offer some clues for the construction of a theory more useful for policy.

The illustrative case used as a vehicle for both aspects of this study is the monopoly power assertedly attained by some firms from excessive persuasive, not necessarily misleading, advertising. This asserted relationship has been subjected to intensive investigation in the United States and Europe for more than twenty years. Stanley I. Ornstein recently presented a critical survey of twenty-three econometric analyses of the effects of advertising.[1] In a high quality study in the mainstream of now conventional theory, William S. Comanor and Thomas A. Wilson go beyond analysis that discovers market failure to estimate its magnitude and to advance diffidently put suggestions for corrective government action.[2] Comanor and Wilson's study serves, therefore, as an appropriate representative of this class of analysis and policy and is in no sense a "straw man." Their tentatively suggested corrective government actions for a "small number" of industries

---

[1] Stanley I. Ornstein, *Industrial Concentration and Advertising Intensity* (Washington, D.C.: American Enterprise Institute, 1977).

[2] William S. Comanor and Thomas A. Wilson, *Advertising and Market Power* (Cambridge, Mass.: Harvard University Press, 1975).

include setting of ceiling prices in regulative proceedings; prevention of price discrimination (quantity discounts) by media; prevention of price discrimination (by size and riskiness of firm) in capital markets; provision of more objective information from sources other than advertising—specifically "information that correctly reported that competing products are equally good or equally useful"; government regulations to require standardization of certain consumer products; limitations on the volume of advertising expenditures either directly or through tax policies or antitrust actions; and elimination or reduction of the lower postal rates for second-class and third-class mail.[3] Such policies applied in behalf of smaller firms and consumers officially found to suffer at the hands of larger firms that garner monopoly profits have obvious political appeal. They also open the way to additional positions of influence and prestige in new or expanded government offices.

There is a clear and present danger that the promised gains are at best illusory because the calculated losses that regulation of advertising and related matters are supposed to mitigate rest on a faulty analysis of the situation and because costs of correction may be greater than any loss they might correct. Nevertheless, the softly put and qualified recommendations may serve the interests of those seeking more regulation, for whatever reason, as well as or better than stronger or better based claims. The process of legislating and building a body of administrative rules tends to transform cautious statements into dogmas and guidelines into straitjackets.

Chapter 2 is a critical examination of the evidence, especially that advanced by Comanor and Wilson, that links advertising to the creation or extension of monopoly power. Comanor and Wilson submit data from forty-one consumer goods industries to a searching econometric analysis. They test a series of hypotheses that associate larger, highly profitable firms in some industries with intensive advertising that erects barriers to competition. The barriers assertedly found by their analysis produce a mix of excessive outlays for advertising, higher costs to smaller firms and entrants (assumed to enter at small scale), and larger profits earned by the larger firms. From these, the extent to which prices are raised to consumers and the loss to misallocation are calculated.

Although provisionally accepting the theory that informs Comanor and Wilson's findings and the correctness of their statistical estimates, this study raises a number of objections: that the amount of sales expense called excessive is exaggerated by being measured from

---

[3]Ibid., pp. 246–53.

the median sales expense of other firms rather than the limit of reasonable advertising expense; that the procedure used to calculate the relationship between advertising and profit overstates the profit by categorizing too much of the advertising as rivalrous (that is, diminishing other firms' assets significantly when successful advertising enhances its own); that the size of price increase to consumers attributable to excessive advertising is overstated because the profit rates of one "small group" used to calculate the price markup due to monopoly is different from the "small group" of excess advertisers; and that the attribution to advertising (except for a parenthetical comment) of all the welfare loss discovered is in error, because substantially more than half is found in industries not characterized as advertising excessively.

If these objections are valid, the size of the welfare loss attributable to advertising in these industries must be a small fraction of the 3.7 percent of value-added in these industries estimated by Comanor and Wilson. All this ignores the possibility that efficiency and consumer welfare may be served better by firms in highly concentrated industries that advertise heavily. It leaves unexamined the possibility that some industries face higher than average risks and so require higher average profits in order to attract capital and wise management.

None of the objections summarized above denies the presence of statistically significant positive correlations between advertising intensity, concentration, and profits. The objections are directed to the interpretation placed upon the relationships and especially on the procedure used to calculate the size of the welfare loss attributable to advertising. Many other investigators find correlations similar to those made by Comanor and Wilson. The interpretation properly placed on them has been a matter of controversy for some time and is well reviewed and tested in Ornstein's book. Chapter 2 of this study makes an assessment of the size of the social cost, if any, associated with intensive advertising. To our knowledge, only Comanor and Wilson have tackled this problem with multiple regression techniques.[4] Consequently, Chapter 2 emphasizes their work.

If the only purpose of this study were to evaluate the welfare loss

---

[4]Other estimates of welfare loss to monopoly that include losses related to advertising exist, but they do not attribute a causal role to advertising. For an evaluation of these studies see the following articles by Dean A. Worcester, Jr.: "Innovations in the Calculation of Welfare Loss to Monopoly," *Western Economic Journal*, vol. 7 (September 1969), pp. 234–43; "New Estimates of the Welfare Loss to Monopoly, United States: 1956–69," *Southern Economic Journal*, vol. 40 (October 1973), pp. 234–45; and "On Monopoly Welfare Losses: Comment," *American Economic Review*, vol. 65 (December 1975), pp. 1015–23. Only the studies that appear to be defective in crucial ways claim to have discovered welfare losses from all sources and for the whole industrial sector as large as those attributed in Comanor and Wilson to excessive advertising by a small group within the forty-one consumer goods industries studied.

attributed to advertising, it would be reasonable to stop at this point or to go on to evaluate a countercase: the theory and data that suggest that economic efficiency (consumer welfare) is better served by large differences in advertising intensity and a variety of industry structures, including concentrated ones subject to no special regulation. But this study has a different, more ambitious objective because it is not reasonable to imagine that any weaknesses in the interpretation of statistically significant connections between advertising, concentration, and inefficiency proclaimed here will seriously deter those who hold with what has been called the "consumer protection" theory of government regulation. For this reason, Chapter 3 examines the corrective actions, listed above, that Comanor and Wilson cautiously advance, against the background of past experience with regulation. The consumer protection theory stands up less well than the producer protection hypothesis. This implies that in time additional government regulation is more likely to close off entry to new competition and to protect existing firms and processes than it is to put consumer welfare first. This in turn suggests that the executives managing existing businesses will not, in the last analysis, resist the imposition of regulation if it is demanded by nonbusiness, or antibusiness, activists.

Regulations put in place in response to nonbusiness or antibusiness pressures acquire a legitimacy that offers business executives an opportunity to gain more control over "their" markets by cooperation with the regulators than is achievable by advertising or other market strategies designed to gain or hold their share of a market at a remunerative price in the face of free entry by other domestic and foreign firms. For this reason, mildly advanced suggestions for more regulation in the name of efficiency and consumer welfare, especially when based upon impressive technical analysis, are likely to have considerable impact even if the size of the statistically computed welfare loss attributable to present conditions is small and the potential overall welfare gain from regulation smaller still, or negative.

The more persuasive theories of regulation analyzed in Chapter 3 are extensions of the normal economic way of thinking. They yield the usual cautious, and generally negative, attitude toward government regulation of markets. Chapter 4 shows why this way of thinking, well designed to explain and predict events, is not well adapted to directing policy. This paradox, noted by the leading figures in economics in the past, exists because inefficiencies and welfare losses are artifacts of *ceteris paribus* assumptions, which disappear when the constrained models essential for the production of testable hypotheses that advance knowledge are replaced by unconstrained models suitable for altering the "real world." In the unconstrained model, changes that would improve the position of all parties will be made as soon as benefits exceed costs to all parties. If changes are not made, it is because the cost of acquiring the necessary information about alternatives is perceived by the affected parties to be too high (and who is to know better?) or else because the cost of working out the appropriate set of rights and duties, or of enforcing them, is greater than the anticipated benefit. Thus the tools that illuminate our knowledge of the economic life inhibit impulses to change it. The key assumption, rational behavior, implies costs of change greater than benefits. This inhibition is heightened by the insight that any change that benefits some people must be expected to harm others, at least in the short run, and we are without a convincing basis whereby we can compare the gain of one to the loss of another unless all agree voluntarily. Otherwise, that kind of judgment is left to a noneconomist elite. Nevertheless, it may be possible to construct some guidelines useful for policy from the materials of economic theory. This is attempted in Chapter 5.

The basic economic theory offers only limited help to policy making because it accepts the basic constraints as given from outside the discipline. It has left to others the task of deciding whether a given preference should be given the weight that the individuals give it, and whether the system of property rights that emerges from contests within the legislative, administrative, and judicial arenas is optimal for individuals. Or rather it has assumed that the balance of persuasion, education, and innate tendencies does produce preferences that have as much, or marginally more, legitimacy than any others and that the set of property rights that has emerged reflects as well as, or a little better than, any other the set of rights that it has been worthwhile to fashion. The contest continues, and all have some role to play in changing the patterns of rights and influencing the preferences, or the range of choices, of others. Changed regulation of advertising, products, and much more may improve the situation in the future, but do economists have any special role to play other than predicting the consequences of alternative changes, and perhaps, asserting strictly personal, and nonscientific, preferences based on their interests? The case that they do is presented in Chapter 5, where our confused and misunderstood theories of rent and profit are clarified and used to define the problem of government regulation. This analysis inevitably focuses attention on basic considerations, but their relevance to advertising and its regulation are eventually made clear.

2

Analysis of Statistical Calculations of Social Losses Attributable to Advertising

A line of economic thought that has long viewed advertising as a cause or at least a symptom of noncompetitive behavior is based on a simplified model of the economic problem. Among its important simplifying assumptions, this model (technically designated "competitive") precludes advertising by assuming that consumers and producers begin with perfect information about products as well as complete knowledge of all buyers and sellers and their bids and offers. By excluding the possibility of ignorance and the selling cost associated with it, the model excludes unavoidable economic tasks and denies the usefulness of much behavior associated with business competition in every context except technical economic literature. It was a small additional step for economists to argue that if advertising was incompatible with this model of perfect competition, it must be associated with a less desirable state of the world—monopoly or monopolistic competition, which misallocates resources, causing a "welfare loss" to consumers.

Reasoning along these lines has been influential especially among economists interested in economic policy. Joan Robinson's[1] description of advertising as a device with which a business can prevent a market from becoming too perfect is treated as axiomatic by such writers as John Kenneth Galbraith, to name only one, who believes that firms successfully engineer consumer demand to fit the qualities of the products they possess.[2] E. H. Chamberlin, in The Theory of Monopolistic Competition, views advertising more as an effect of monopolistic elements.[3] Either way, prices to consumers are increased

---

[1]Joan Robinson, The Economics of Imperfect Competition (London: Macmillan, 1933).

[2]John Kenneth Galbraith, The Affluent Society (Boston: Houghton Mifflin, 1958), pp. 155–56.

[3]E. H. Chamberlin, The Theory of Monopolistic Competition (Cambridge, Mass.: Harvard University Press, 1933), p. 129.

by the cost of advertising. Both viewpoints can be found in recent writings of economists in the Federal Trade Commission.[4]

The idea that advertising could become a barrier to entry received strong support from Nicholas Kaldor and Joe S. Bain in the early 1950s.[5] Their studies provide most of the limited theoretical basis found in many of the writings of more recent critics of advertising. These barriers-to-entry arguments are never completely clear, but the general notion suggests either economies of scale in advertising (placing smaller firms at a disadvantage) or cumulative effects of past and present advertising (forcing heavy capital costs onto potential new entrants). Diligent analysis has not established either basis for monopoly by advertising. Yet even if they were established beyond question, it does not follow that economic efficiency, or the consumer, would be better served by different arrangements. Cogent defenses of this type cannot prevent the indictment of advertising, indeed it was made long ago, but careful analysis may display its merits and lead to a favorable verdict.

Recent critics of advertising have attempted to test the possible relationship between advertising and resource misallocation indirectly by empirically examining the relationship between advertising intensity and three proxies for monopoly. Monopoly is assumed to be present if the largest four (or eight) firms produce a large proportion of industry output, if firms enjoy higher than average profit rates, or if the ratio between price and cost seems large. These measures are suspect tests of resource misallocation because they rest on the unstated easy assumption that more efficient alternatives exist. Those in a position to change things should not overlook the possibility that the degree of concentration, the rate of profits, and the margins of price over cost may reflect real economies and efficient adjustment to risk.[6] Nevertheless, statistically significant positive relationships between advertising, concentration, above average profit rates, and/or price-cost margins lead some economists to assert a cause and effect relationship, running from advertising to monopoly, that wastes resources and harms consumers.

A 1967 paper by H. M. Mann, J. A. Henning, and J. W. Meehan,

---

[4]See, for instance, Kellogg Company, General Mills Inc., General Foods Corporation, The Quaker Oats Company. Complaint, Docket No. 8883, Federal Trade Commission, April 26, 1972.

[5]Nicholas Kaldor, "The Economic Aspects of Advertising," *Review of Economic Studies*, vol. 18 (1949–1950), pp. 1–27; and Joe S. Bain, *Barriers to New Competition* (Cambridge, Mass.: Harvard University Press, 1956).

[6]For a critical appraisal of the use of concentration ratios, profitability, or price-cost margins to observe or measure resource misallocation, see John S. McGee, *In Defense of Industrial Concentration* (New York: Praeger, 1971).

Jr., is an influential example of this view.[7] This paper supplied the critics of advertising with some evidence on which to base policy recommendations about limiting advertising. There has developed recently a body of literature that is critical of the Mann, Henning, and Meehan methodology; another that does not confirm this supposed relationship; and still another that recognizes the relationship but, following Chamberlin, argues the reverse line of causation, that is, that concentration causes more intensive advertising.[8] However, reviewing the literature available in 1970, F. M. Scherer concluded,

> Intensive advertising can also raise barriers to the entry of new competition permitting producers to enjoy for extended periods of time monopoly profits commensurate with their power over prices. Thus *high prices, waste, income distribution* in favor of stock holders and *misallocation of resources* are the consequences of excessive image differentiation.[9]

The Federal Trade Commission apparently accepts Scherer's conclusion. Nor is it hesitant to cite Mann in its recent attack on "brand dominance" of ReaLemon. According to the FTC, this dominance was acquired by product differentiation and advertising used by ReaLemon to build barriers to entry that have allowed it to advance prices over cost.[10] Clearly, advertising studies are not mere ivory tower exercises. At least those hostile to advertising are being used officially to support policies to restrict this aspect of free speech and to magnify the influ-

---

[7]H. M. Mann, J. A. Henning, and J. W. Meehan, Jr., "Advertising and Concentration: An Empirical Investigation," *Journal of Industrial Economics*, vol. 16 (November 1967), pp. 34–45. For a rejoinder and a discussion of their results, see Robert B. Ekelund, Jr., and Charles Maurice, "Symposium on Advertising and Concentration," *Journal of Industrial Economics*, vol. 18, no. 1 (November 1969), pp. 76–101.

[8]For a review of both the theoretical and empirical literature on advertising, see Ornstein, *Industrial Concentration and Advertising Intensity*. He also retests the supposed advertising-concentration relationship, finding the relationship to be weak and probably spurious. Also see Yale Brozen, "Entry Barriers: Advertising and Product Differentiation," in Harvey J. Goldschmid, H. Michael Mann, and J. Fred Weston, eds., *Industrial Concentration: The New Learning* (Boston: Little, Brown, 1974), pp. 115–37. For a review more sympathetic to studies linking concentration and advertising, see H. Michael Mann, "Advertising, Concentration and Profitability: The State of Knowledge and Directions for Public Policy," in Goldschmid et al., *Industrial Concentration*, pp. 137–56. For a slightly more technical review of the literature, see James M. Ferguson, *Advertising and Competition: Theory, Measurement, Fact* (Cambridge, Mass.: Ballinger, 1975). Among the recent supporters for the advertising-concentration relation is Allyn D. Strickland and Leonard W. Weiss, "Advertising, Concentration, and Price-Cost Margins," *Journal of Political Economy*, vol. 84 (October 1976), pp. 1109–21. Also see the proceedings of an American Enterprise Institute conference, *Issues in Advertising: The Economics of Persuasion* (Washington, D.C.: American Enterprise Institute, 1978).

[9]F. M. Scherer, *Industrial Market Structure and Economic Performance* (Chicago: Rand McNally, 1970), p. 344 (italics added).

[10]Borden Inc., Case, Docket No. 8978, Federal Trade Commission, August 19, 1976.

9

ence of government agencies even when no issue of truthfulness of statement or effectiveness of product is present.

This chapter assesses research that associates advertising with the social losses mentioned by Scherer. The first and only econometric effect to isolate and estimate the magnitude of these losses known to us appears in William S. Comanor and Thomas A. Wilson's *Advertising and Market Power.*[11] Their investigation represents the present limit of what can be done to establish the connection they believe to exist between advertising and market power, and the significance of this connection for welfare. They also offer tentative suggestions, some of which possess political appeal, that in their view mitigate the social losses. Thus their work is examined as an example of the quality and the vigor of support for the hypothesis that excess advertising causes social loss and to evaluate the accuracy of their estimates of the size of social loss and the appropriateness of their suggestions for improved government policy to remedy any perceived deficiencies.

Comanor and Wilson's book is a sophisticated empirical investigation similar in many ways to other empirical studies that uncover statistically significant relationships between advertising concentration and profits. They offer an advertising-as-a-barrier-to-entry theory of monopoly and welfare loss to society and to consumers. They conclude:

> The total effect of advertising is larger than the figure shown for excess advertising itself, since advertising affects profit margins, thereby giving rise to allocative inefficiency and monopoly transfers. In addition, these higher price-cost margins contribute to technical inefficiency by permitting firms of suboptimal size to exist.[12]

This study argues that the existence of barriers damaging to efficiency and consumer welfare is unproved, that the mildly stated corrections advanced in Comanor and Wilson's final chapter stand a good chance of becoming part of the regulatory system imposed by courts, administrative agencies, and perhaps legislatures, and that if this should come to pass, the losses to society, and especially to consumers, will be far larger than the gains.

Advertising as a Basis for Welfare Loss to Monopoly

Comanor and Wilson hold that barriers to entry, a necessity for monopoly power, are created because smaller firms and new firms

---

[11]Comanor and Wilson, *Advertising and Market Power.*
[12]Ibid., p. 244.

must incur high market penetration costs imposed by such things as quantity discounts for television advertisements. Market penetration costs are considered to be higher for small existing firms and for potential entrants than for the large existing firms because large existing firms can blanket a given market with a variety of products (product differentiation) and advertise them effectively at lower cost per unit of sales than can small existing firms and potential entrants. Thus the large firms have a cost advantage for marketing any given quality of product, plus a further advantage because the consumer may be misled to associate higher quality with the more highly advertised product even though the quality may be no higher than for products of the small firms. In addition, larger firms are thought to have economies of scale in production.

Comanor and Wilson subject all these relationships to econometric tests. Regressions are run to determine if quantity discounts are available to larger purchasers of television advertising. Additional regressions are used to test relationships between advertising, profit rates, and concentration. They then defend their treatment of advertising as an expense, rather than as an investment, and finally they undertake calculations of possible welfare losses, and transfers from consumers to monopolists, associated with advertising and market power.

Comanor and Wilson limit their ambitious analysis in important and defensible ways. Their basic data are from Internal Revenue Service statistics for forty-one manufacturing industries that produce consumer goods. These represent broad definitions of industries, approximately equivalent to the three-digit classification used by the Department of Commerce. Only firms producing predominantly for the consumer market are included; other producers are usually reached more efficiently by other selling techniques. Only manufactured goods are included in an effort to obtain a more homogeneous statistical population. Some of the limitations are unfortunate necessities. The only sales expense considered is advertising because this is the only form for which data were available. Apparently only advertising placed by firms in newspapers, magazines, radio, and television is included, but mail order and other types may also be included. Not all advertising is counted because firms that produce their own advertising, rather than dealing with agencies, may have accounted for it under some category unrelated to any specific function.

The basic data are for the years 1954–1957. The general approach is to examine cross sections of the data, usually across all firms in a given industry. At the conclusion, virtually all the misallocation seems to be attributed to unidentified small groups among the forty-one industries

Table 1
Profits and Advertising-Sales Ratios

Industry	Advertising-Sales Ratio (percent)	Profits[a] (percent)	(rank)[b]
1. Perfumes[c]	15.3	13.5	4
2. Cereals	10.3	14.8	2
3. Drugs[c]	9.9	14.0	3
4. Soaps	9.2	11.7	6.5
5. Malt liquors	6.8	7.2	24
6. Soft drinks	6.2	10.0	14
7. Clocks and watches	5.6	1.9	38
8. Wines	5.2	7.3	22.5
9. Cigarettes	4.8	11.5	8
10. Hand tools	4.2	11.4	9
11. Costume jewelry	4.0	1.4	40
12. Electrical appliances	3.5	10.3	11
13. Confectionery	3.5	10.6	10
14. Jewelry	3.2	5.3	31.5
15. Canning	2.9	6.4	26
16. Bakery products	2.9	9.3	17.5
17. Cigars	2.6	5.3	31.5
18. Books[c]	2.4	10.1	13
19. Dairy products	2.2	7.9	20
20. Hats	2.2	1.6	39
21. Radio, TV, and phonograph	2.2	8.8	19
22. Distilled liquors[c]	2.1	5.0	34
23. Carpets	2.0	4.5	36
24. Instruments	2.0	12.0	5
25. Grain mill products	1.9	7.0	25

studied, alternatively eight or eleven of the forty-one, depending on the advertising-to-sales ratio selected as the lower bound for excessive. One of the eight with the highest advertising-to-sales ratio had a low profit rate, as did one of the three additional industries in the next highest group. The industries are listed in Table 1 in order of their advertising-to-sales ratio. The rank order of the industry profits is given in the right-hand column. The same data are displayed in Figure 1, a scattergram relating advertising-to-sales ratios to profit rates. The vertical dashed line separates from the others the eight industries said to have excessively high advertising-to-sales ratios plus the other three with somewhat excessive ratios. The average profit rates for four subgroups are depicted by horizontal lines. The four groups are the

Table 1 (Continued)

Industry	Advertising-Sales Ratio (percent)	Profits[a] (percent)	(rank)[b]
26. Household and service machinery (nonelectrical)	1.9	7.3	22.5
27. Women's clothing	1.8	6.1	27
28. Screens and blinds	1.6	9.3	17.5
29. Furniture	1.5	9.7	16
30. Footwear	1.5	7.6	21
31. Paints[c]	1.5	9.9	15
32. Tires and tubes	1.4	10.2	12
33. Knit goods	1.3	3.8	37
34. Men's clothing	1.2	5.9	28
35. Motorcycles and bicycles	1.1	5.2	33
36. Furs	1.0	5.7	30
37. Millinery	0.8	−1.3	41
38. Meat	0.6	4.6	35
39. Motor vehicles[c]	0.6	15.5	1
40. Sugar	0.2	5.8	29
41. Periodicals[c]	0.2	11.7	6.5

Note: Industries with advertising-sales ratios greater than 5.0 are considered to have excessive advertising according to Comanor and Wilson, who also calculate the costs under a more relaxed definition of excessive advertising, using 4.0 as the limit of "normal" advertising.
[a] "Profits" are profits after taxes as a percentage of equity.
[b] This number is the rank order in terms of profit rates.
[c] Industries in a group of seven found to meet the test applied for economies of scale in advertising.
Source: William S. Comanor and Thomas A. Wilson, *Advertising and Market Power* (Cambridge, Mass.: Harvard University Press, 1975), table 6.A.2, pp. 134–35.

thirty with "reasonable" advertising intensity, the three with moderately excessive intensity, the next four, and the four with the highest intensity as measured by the advertising-to-sales ratio (total industry advertising expense expressed as a percentage of industry sales).

General Procedures for Calculating Loss to Monopoly. Three categories of losses to misallocation are hypothesized by Comanor and Wilson: the cost of excess advertising itself; less efficient production because some firms are kept too small by the advertising of the larger firms and so have higher than necessary costs of production; and deadweight loss due to the restricted production of the advertising

Figure 1
Scattergram of the Basic Data

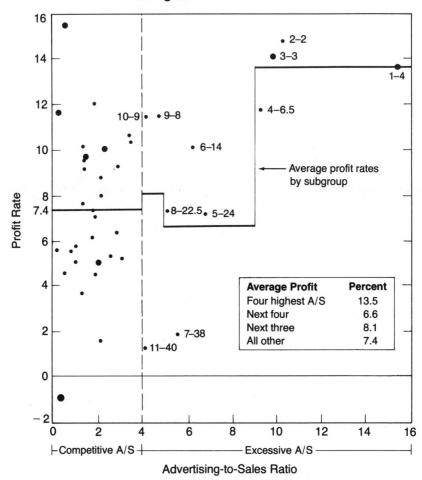

Note: The pairs of numbers give the rank orders of advertising-to-sales ratios and profit rates for the eleven industries with the highest advertising-to-sales ratios.

● = the industry with a negative profit rate (millinery).

• = industries found by Comanor and Wilson to enjoy economies of scale in advertising.

group as a whole that displaces resources to activities less valued by consumers. For convenience these will be referred to as losses to advertising, to inefficiency, and to deadweight loss. For the whole sample, the largest loss is attributed by Comanor and Wilson to suboptimal capacities of the smaller firms and the intermediate loss to excessive advertising itself. Deadweight losses are small. In addition, they find a transfer from consumers in the form of profits that are equal to

14

about two-thirds of the total misallocation losses.[13] The method of calculating each cost is somewhat arbitrary.

Figure 2 illustrates the losses implied by Comanor and Wilson for a small number of industries where economies of scale of advertising have resulted in welfare loss. The example supposes half the output to be from small firms found in Comanor and Wilson's econometrics to have high production costs and also high advertising costs per unit of output because they have not penetrated the market sufficiently to

Figure 2

Social Losses and Transfers to Profits Due to Excessive Advertising

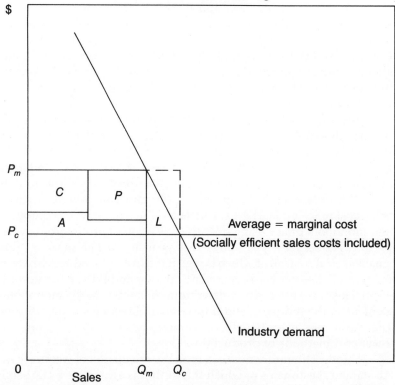

Note: Social losses are assertedly the sum of the excessive advertising expenditure by all sizes of firms, higher costs of production imposed on the smaller firms, and the net loss of values to consumers—illustrated by areas $A + C + L$. Smaller firms make no monopoly profit, but larger firms do, giving them a transfer income at the expense of consumers. Consumers' surplus is reduced, therefore, by the whole area $A + C + L + P$, it is said.

---

[13]Ibid., p. 242.

achieve low costs per unit. They are assumed to make only normal profits (no monopoly return) because of higher costs. Advertising is assumed to raise prices from the competitive level P_c to the monopoly level P_m. Much of the increase is dissipated in higher costs: higher advertising costs to all firms in the industry (area A), higher costs of production for smaller firms (area C), and deadweight loss (area L). Additionally, there is a transfer from consumers in the form of profits to the excessive advertisers (area P). The three areas (A, C, and L) are social losses by this interpretation. The task Comanor and Wilson set for themselves can be stated as an effort to determine the size of these areas plus the size of transfer to the larger firms that garner profits from excessive advertising.

The four areas, A, C, L, and P, are all drawn in Figure 2 on the assumption that the excess advertising does not shift the demand curve further to the right. This assumption is, apparently, adopted by Comanor and Wilson although their data reveal a substantial relationship between relative industrywide expenditures on advertising and industry sales. This critically important assumption is analyzed in the final section of this chapter.

This analysis is in a major branch of the mainstream that originated with Arnold C. Harberger's 1954 article.[14] It differs in two important ways from Harberger's interpretation. It ascribes a deadweight loss to part of the rectangular area inclusive of A, P, and C, and it adds advertising and higher production costs to profits per unit to determine the difference between monopoly and competitive price (the price-cost margin). Harberger calculated the gap between competitive and monopoly prices using only the deviation of profits from average profits. Harberger's procedure results in a smaller markup and a smaller social cost, all of which is registered in a reduced area like area L in Figure 2. Neither Harberger nor Comanor and Wilson treat profit as a social loss because it is a transfer from consumers to the monopolistic element in the industry, and it has only indirect effects on efficiency. The profit may even benefit consumers, by, for example, financing lower cost methods of production.

A modest literature now exists on the calculation of welfare losses. All statistical estimates of which this author is aware use a Harberger-style approach to measure L-type areas illustrated in Figure 2. The logic underlying these calculations is straightforward. Resources excluded by monopolists, who produce output Q_m rather than Q_c, produce goods of value in other industries. The value of these goods is given by the area under the marginal cost curve, here assumed (as it nearly

---

[14]Arnold C. Harberger, "Monopoly and Resource Allocation," *American Economic Review*, vol. 44 (May 1954), pp. 77–87.

always is) to be horizontal. But the value added to the satisfaction of consumer wants in the industry under consideration is measured by the area under its demand curve. Therefore, the *net* loss for society, the "welfare loss" from continued monopoly, is equal to area *L*.

Harberger's analysis had a subtlety that was not matched by some writers. Recognizing that a general equilibrium model is necessary to discuss, even crudely, a welfare loss to society, he chose a competitive profit rate that matched restricted outputs in some (monopolistic) industries with overextended output in others. Approximately as much welfare loss appeared in each set of industries. Other writers, perhaps shocked by the trivial welfare loss calculated by Harberger, not so carefully produced estimates based on the hidden assumption that all industries could expand output, apparently not recognizing the excessive demand that this placed on the total amount of resources available. This literature is reviewed in two articles, one of which includes an effort to find the upper limit of defensible estimates by deliberately biasing the data and procedures at every turn to make the welfare loss as high as possible. Although this estimate is about seven times larger than Harberger's, it is still only about one percent of GNP. [15]

Challenges to the limitation of the welfare loss to the "Harberger triangle" began with Gordon Tullock's 1968 paper; it has been substantially advanced by Richard A. Posner. [16] Comanor and Wilson pursue this general line of argument. It is, perhaps, a watershed in the econometric calculation of welfare loss to monopolistic concentration. As already stated, Harberger's approach treats profits as transfers only tangentially related to efficiency. They are used to find the price increase attributed to monopoly, but the profits themselves are neutral. Tullock and Posner see them as stimuli that will cause enterprisers to

---

[15]Worcester, "Innovations in the Calculation of Welfare Loss to Monopoly," and "New Estimates of the Welfare Loss to Monopoly." Even the small losses found by Harberger can be persuasively attacked as too high. Yale Brozen, in a private communication, gives data on some of the industries shown by Harberger to contribute the largest losses. But when additional (smaller) firms are included, the (low) profits reported by Harberger are found to be unrepresentative of the industry. My estimates used data for the 500 largest industrial firms reported in the *Fortune* surveys for the years 1956–1969, thereby including short-run disequilibrium deviations with monopolistic distortion. The use of data on firms, rather than industries, attempted to ferret out monopolies that were submerged in broad classifications of "industries," and an effort was made to separate the firms according to degree of conglomerateness. Additionally, the price termed competitive was low, and the loss found for these large industries was assumed to be typical of the whole output of the nation.

[16]Gordon Tullock, "The Welfare Costs of Tariffs, Monopoly and Theft," *Western Economic Journal*, vol. 5 (June 1967), pp. 224–32; Richard A. Posner, "The Social Cost of Monopoly and Regulation," *Journal of Political Economy*, vol. 83 (August 1975), pp. 807–27.

expend real resources approximately equal in value to the monopoly profit in order to get their share. In Harberger's analysis, resources excluded from the monopolized industries produce useful goods in competitive (or less monopolistic) sectors. In Posner's analysis, free enterprise ensures freedom to attempt to monopolize, but equally the freedom to use resources to compete with monopolists. One might say that seeking monopoly is a competitive business, with everyone's ability to secure a monopoly limited by the desire of everyone else to share any monopoly others may have achieved.

According to Tullock and Posner's view, the resources that a monopolist does not use for production of goods and services are not, as Harberger would have it, merely transferred to the production of other goods and services of value to consumers. Instead, they are used up in the production of defensive advertising by the monopolist; aggressive advertising by his rivals; efforts of the monopolist to establish and defend patents, to secure favorable and to fend off unfavorable laws and regulations, and to innovate a range of product types and styles that leave few interstices for would-be competitors. At the same time, their rivals spend resources to counter and overcome these defensive moves, not all of which are beneficial to consumers and some of which reduce total output. Additional resources are employed to expand each of these activities, and others, until the last dollar spent in each direction yields the same return. The number of rivals in the industry increases until the average return is no more than in any other industry after absorbing true costs. At a maximum, the whole area is absorbed in elevated costs and monopoly transfers, areas A, C, and P in Figure 2. Posner, however, includes only the profit area in estimating the amount of deadweight losses associated with the rectangular area. He computes deadweight loss equal to 3.4 percent of GNP using Harberger's data.

The historical word for the activity stimulated by the lure of profit has been "competition." Posner agrees that such activity confers benefits on consumers, but he chooses to ignore this aspect because he believes that the gains will be less than the cost, and in any case he wishes to confine himself to "methods of monopolizing which have little or no social value."[17] This line of reasoning is, however, paradoxical and even contradictory. Quite aside from the arbitrary exclusion of all socially beneficial innovation and quality improvement stimulated by efforts to create or break into temporary monopoly positions, one must be skeptical about any important tendency for observed profits to measure the value of resources expended for such purposes. Nor can one be confident of the direction of the error. Far more may be spent. It

---

[17]Posner, "Social Cost of Monopoly and Regulation," p. 811.

is said that virtually no one in the rush to the Klondike covered their expenses. Or it may be much less. Superior ball point pens broke the initial monopoly price in less than two years.

In any case, the absence of profits is a useless indicator of efficiency if the Posner view is accepted. Costs dissipated in rivalry are costs, and, however great, they will not be discovered by looking at profit data. When such costs exist, they diminish (perhaps to zero) both the rectangular profit area and the monopoly markup, which provides the base for calculating the triangular area. What is needed to avoid this paradox is a measure of the monopoly markup that is independent of profits, one that instead measures wasteful advertising, product development, and other expenses part or all of which may be absorbed in constructing monopolies or countering rivals in ways not beneficial to consumers.

Comanor and Wilson's approach, by accident or design, avoids this trap by seeking more direct measures of wasteful expenses. Their first problem must be to find some way to distinguish excessive from socially desirable amounts of advertising (area A in Figure 2). According to their expectations, the larger firms will spend more than the socially needed amount for advertising and the smaller firms will be forced to spend an even larger amount per unit of sales to overcome threshold and brand loyalty effects and quantity discounts that favor the larger firms in their industry. Exceptions found by Comanor and Wilson's analysis are discussed later in this chapter.

Next, they must calculate the extent to which costs of production by disadvantaged firms are raised because excessive advertising of others prevents them from achieving economies of scale. This provides a base for an estimate of area C in Figure 2. This area represents the higher cost of production assertedly suffered by the smaller firms. They earn normal profits at the monopoly price, but they are inefficiently small. The larger firms earn profits that the smaller ones, presumably, cannot compete away.

An estimated elasticity of demand is needed to calculate area L because it depends upon the amount sales are reduced in response to the higher "monopoly" price inferred from the cost-raising advertising and its consequences. The importance of elasticity for this calculation is apparent from Figure 2. At one extreme the demand curve would be vertical. In that case there is no misallocation because the amount demanded does not increase at a lower price, so the area L is zero. The larger the elasticity, the larger the loss. In principle, the loss would be infinitely large if elasticity were so high that consumers wanted more of the product than could be produced with all of the world's resources at the competitive price. But in that case the monopolist would make far larger profits than he does by expanding his output, unless he already employed all of society's resources. Abram Bergson pursues a sophisticated form of this analysis and presents tables showing very large losses, as much as 40 percent of national income.[18] The large losses, however, are inconsistent with all statistical estimations of demand elasticities, and, even more remarkably, with profit-maximizing behavior on the part of the monopolists.[19] Comanor and Wilson's approach is far more relevant than Bergson's to the advancement of understanding.

Cost of advertising. Some valuable information is most economically conveyed by advertising. The socially desirable amount varies with the type of product, the dispersion of customers, and other factors. There is, however, little theory to explain socially valuable differences in interindustry advertising intensities. It is, therefore, arbitrary to designate some amount as excessive. It is also essential to the whole investigation. Comanor and Wilson decide to determine the threshold beyond which excess advertising is said to exist from two observations: the skewness of the distribution of advertising-to-sales ratios among industries producing consumer goods, and the strength of the influence between advertising-to-sales ratios and profit rates on investment.[20] Two cutoff levels are chosen: advertising-to-sales ratios alternatively of 4 percent and 5 percent. The advertising-to-sales ratio for each industry that is excessive is then found by subtracting the *mean* value of the advertising-to-sales ratios for all industries *below* the critical level from the actual ratio for industries that advertise excessively. This is then multiplied by actual sales expenditures to give the dollar amount of excessive advertising in each industry.

The basis for determining the ratio beyond which "excessive" advertising exists is open to question. Most of Comanor and Wilson's group of excessive advertisers are in industries where novelty is important to consumers, the cost of production is relatively low, and the purchases are frequent. In these industries the possibility apparently exists to use advertising to help detach enough purchasers from rivals to make the expenditures worthwhile. The "optimal" amount of advertising in these industries with rapid product turnover might well be different than in those with infrequently purchased, more mundane

[18] Abram Bergson, "On Monopoly Welfare Losses," *American Economic Review,* vol. 63 (December 1973), pp. 863–70.

[19] Worcester, "On Monopoly Welfare Losses: Comment"; and Richard Hartman, "On Monopoly Welfare Losses, Once Again," *Economic Inquiry,* vol. 16 (April 1978), pp. 293–302.

[20] Comanor and Wilson, *Advertising and Market Power,* p. 240.

products. Without explanation of the expected type of distribution, what can be made of a nonnormal one?

Comanor and Wilson take the existence of a strong positive correlation between advertising and profit rates as evidence that advertising above some level is excessive. This correlation is found by others to break down when advertising is treated as an investment that produces lasting values. This is discussed later in this chapter.

Cost of suboptimal capacity. The second large cost obtained by Comanor and Wilson is attributable to smaller firms operating at high costs while sheltered by high price-cost margins of larger firms. Comanor and Wilson estimate this cost for all forty-one industries although it appears out of place in their argument for the thirty-three industries found not to engage in excessive advertising. In those industries with advertising-to-sales ratios below the critical level, this cost must be attributed to undefined causes other than advertising. This turns out to be four-fifths of the total loss attributed to suboptimal capacity.

The argument associating higher costs for smaller firms with inefficiency and loss to consumers in any of the forty-one industries is weak because it ignores the diversity within the industries, the size and density of geographical regions within the United States, and the variety of production techniques and factor endowments. Thus, smaller "higher-cost" firms producing a more specialized product, or for a limited geographical market, may have a comparative advantage. Or managers whose earnings come from profits—while earning less because they are less able than rivals—nevertheless earn more than they could elsewhere. Either of these conditions could explain what Comanor and Wilson's approach cannot: the continued existence of smaller, "inefficient" firms that seemingly could be profitably pushed to the wall by the larger firms. But if the diversity of firm sizes and apparent costs reflect efficient adaptation to diverse real conditions, the presence of the smaller high cost firms holds prices down better than any known alternative. When many nonidentical products sold in a very large, diverse market are assembled into only forty-one categories, as is the case here, diversity of many types, including size of firm and cost-price ratios, cannot be accepted as evidence of inefficiency without substantial supporting analysis. Still, if there are economies of scale in advertising, some unnecessarily high cost production may occur.

Deadweight loss in allocative efficiency. The deadweight loss is the cost to society of producing too little of the goods in the heavily advertised sector. For this to happen, the value to the consumer must not be increased by the advertising. If it is, it will show up as a rightward shift of the demand curve for the industry as a whole. For the time being, a fixed demand curve is assumed, but it turns out to be inconsistent with Comanor and Wilson's statistical findings and will therefore be examined carefully in a later section of this chapter.

As already noted, Comanor and Wilson use basically the same method other economists have used to calculate conventional dead-weight loss, L in Figure 2. It requires a numerical estimate of the elasticity of demand and of the difference between competitive and monopoly prices. They go beyond other writers to calculate separate demand elasticities for each of the forty-one industries. Their way of estimating the price-cost margin has already been described in a general way. More details are given below. However, the costs associated with misallocation are not large.

Monopoly transfer. Monopoly transfer is calculated by estimating the difference between a calculated competitive rate of profit and the actual rate, multiplied by the value of sales. While the monopoly transfer of profits is not said to represent a loss to society, it does represent a transfer from some individuals (consumers) to other individuals (generally, owners). Thus all decisions about the social usefulness of differences in sales and production costs affect the size of the estimate.

Comanor and Wilson's Results. Table 2 displays the estimates of the cost of market power that were obtained by Comanor and Wilson using both 4 percent and 5 percent as the maximum "normal" levels of advertising.

If 5 percent is chosen, over half the loss is in industries *other than those with excess advertising,* specifically, 84.8 percent of the cost of suboptimal capacity, 55.7 percent of the conventional deadweight losses (allocative inefficiency), and 86.2 percent of monopoly transfer. All the loss due directly to excess advertising expense is, of course, attributed to the eight industries said to advertise excessively. Excessive advertising itself accounts for 67.1 percent of all loss to consumers by the eight industries that are said to advertise monopolistically but only 25.2 percent of overall loss. The Harberger-type loss is only 5.4 percent of the total loss, three-tenths of one percent of value-added in these industries.

The larger loss, 62.4 percent of the total, which was found in the industries that do not advertise excessively, prompted Comanor and Wilson to note that the "relative losses due to suboptimal capacity and the value of monopoly transfers is not very different for these subsets of industries than for the sector as a whole. This reflects the fact that *other sources* of market power are important among some of the remain-

Table 2
Asserted Costs of Market Power
(dollar amounts in millions)

Source of Estimated Loss	5% Critical Level						4% Critical Level					
	Cost to consumer						Cost to consumer					
	All consumer goods		Excessive advertisers only		Difference[a]		All consumer goods		Excessive advertisers only		Difference[a]	
Excess advertising	$ 656	25.2%	$656	67.1%	$ 0	0.0%	$827	29.3%	$ 827	62.7%	$ 0	0.0%
Cost of suboptimal capacity	736	28.3	112	11.5	624	84.8	736	26.1	156	11.8	580	78.8
Loss of allocative efficiency	140	5.4	62	6.3	78	55.7	161	5.7	90	6.8	71	44.1
Total cost to society	1532	58.9	830	84.9	702	45.8	1724	61.0	1073	81.3	651	37.8
Monopoly transfer	1070	41.1	148	15.1	922	86.2	1100	39.0	247	18.7	853	77.5
Total cost to consumers	2602	100.0	978	100.0	1624	62.4	2824	100.0	1320	100.0	1504	53.3

[a] Amount and percent not in industries with excessive advertising.

Source: Computed from data given in Comanor and Wilson, *Advertising and Market Power*, tables 11.1 and 11.2, pp. 242, 244.

ing consumer goods manufacturing industries."[21] They do not consider the effect of this finding on the theoretical foundation for their analysis.

Analysis of Comanor and Wilson's Findings

Comanor and Wilson's analysis raises many theoretical and statistical issues.[22] Some can be discussed in a paragraph or two; others require extended discussion. The length of treatment is unrelated to the size of the welfare loss asserted, and it tends to be confusing because the issues are interrelated. Clarity is sought by organizing our commentary according to the source of the welfare loss. Thus criticism of losses charged against excessive advertising are taken up first, then those attributed to overly small firm size, followed by losses to consumers consequent upon the monopoly transfer, and finally some general points including the calculation of the conventional deadweight welfare loss.

Advertising as a Barrier to Entry: Which "Small Group?" The basic thesis tested by Comanor and Wilson is that larger firms can establish and preserve some measure of profitable monopoly power by excessive amounts of advertising—excessive in the sense that it goes beyond the amounts needed to inform and instruct potential consumers to levels that override valuable efforts by rivals to get a favorable reception for equally good products. This is at times said to rest on economies of scale in advertising, presumably revealed in a lower advertising cost per unit of sales by the larger, more profitable firms.

Comanor and Wilson investigate the existence of economies of scale in advertising by comparing four-firm and eight-firm concentration ratios of advertising, sales, and assets. According to the critics of advertising, if economies of scale in advertising exist, the largest four (or eight) firms will need to spend less for advertising as a proportion of their sales or assets than will the smaller firms. This will be revealed by a comparison of the proportion of industry expenditures by the largest four (or eight) for advertising with their share of industry assets or of

---

[21]Ibid., p. 245 (italics added).

[22]A book by Jean-Jacques Lambin, *Advertising, Competition, and Market Conduct in Oligopoly over Time* (Amsterdam, New York: North-Holland/Elsevier, 1976) came to our attention too late to be given as much attention as it deserves in this study. It is particularly valuable because its intensive econometric analysis is based on competition among brands of close substitutes. It provides a more cogent comparison test of the advertising-as-a-barrier-to-entry hypothesis than does a comparison of difference among broadly defined "industries." Lambin's approach and conclusions are reported here, but they have not been subjected to close scrutiny.

Table 3

Advertising–Sales Ratios, Profit Rates, Elasticities of Advertising and Price: The Eight and the Seven

Industry	Advertising-Sales Ratio (percent)	Profit Rate (percent)	Elasticities	
			Advertising (long run)	Price (long run)
The eight:				
Soft drinks	6.2	10.0	.591	−1.540
Malt liquors	6.8	7.2	.010	−1.392
Wines	5.2	7.3	1.202	−0.842
Cereals	10.3	14.8	.320[a]	−2.099[a]
Soaps	9.2	11.7	.294	−0.784
Clocks and watches	5.6	1.9	.583	−9.802
Drugs	9.9	14.0	1.042	−1.695
Perfumes	15.3	13.5	.013	+0.287
The seven:				
Drugs	9.9	14.0	1.042	−1.695
Perfumes	15.3	13.5	.013	+0.287
Distilled liquors	2.1	5.0	.745	−0.295
Periodicals	0.2	11.7	.013	−0.363
Books	2.4	10.1	.348	−1.078
Paints	1.5	9.9	—	—
Motor vehicles	0.6	15.5	.000	0.000
Average of the eight heaviest advertisers	8.6	10.1	.507	−2.590[b]
Average of the seven with economies of scale in advertising	4.6	11.4	.360	−0.686[b]
Average of the seven, omitting the overlap with the eight	1.4	10.4	.277	−0.434
Average of the other industries	3.1	8.4	.477	−0.846

[a] Grain mill plus cereals.
[b] Positive elasticities are omitted from this simple average. If the improbably high elasticity for clocks and watches is also omitted from the eight, the unweighted average is −1.392.

Sources: All from Comanor and Wilson, *Advertising and Market Power:* columns 1 and 2—table 6.A.2, pp. 134–35; columns 3 and 4—table 5.8, pp. 89–90; identification of the eight with the largest advertising-sales ratios—table 6.A; identification of the seven with economies of scale in advertising by their test—table 9.1, pp. 199–200, and table 9.2, p. 201.

sales.[23] Ten industries have these characteristics if four-firm concentra-

---

[23]Figure 2 is relevant to the small group of seven where the cost of advertising per unit of output is lower for the larger firms. In the usual case, including six of the eight with the highest advertising-to-sales ratios, the larger firms spent as much or more per unit of sales.

tion ratios are used, seven if both four and eight are used; Comanor and Wilson choose the latter. The seven industries found by this procedure to enjoy economies of scale in advertising are drugs, perfumes, distilled liquors, periodicals, books, paints, and motor vehicles. Only the first two have advertising to sales ratios found elsewhere by Comanor and Wilson to be excessive. A comparison of the two groups is given in Table 3 and also in Table 1 and Figure 2. The larger firms are declared to have an advantage because of quantity discounts for TV time and for other media. Only TV is investigated by Comanor and Wilson.

Comanor and Wilson analyze the small group of seven without calling attention to the fact that only two, perfumes and drugs, of the eight industries with high advertising-to-sales ratios attributable to advertising make this list. Examination of the two lists of industries, the seven and the eight, is damaging to their conclusion:

> Thus we conclude that larger firms typically have *higher* advertising:sales ratios than their smaller rivals *except* where advertising is a particularly important feature of industry behavior. In these industries, available evidence suggests that the leading firms spend *less* than their rivals.[24]

Two matters are at issue here, the accuracy of this statement and the significance of admission that typically the larger firms have the larger advertising-to-sales ratios. It is true that *on the average,* the seven industries in which large firms spend less per unit of output on advertising than their smaller competitors also have rather high advertising-to-sales ratios, "4.6 percent," in contrast to the average of the others,[25] but as is evident from the advertising-to-sales ratio column of Table 3, this would not be so without the inclusion of the two industries, drugs and perfumes, which also appear among the eight. Without them the average advertising-to-sales ratio lies *below* the average of the others, given by Comanor and Wilson as 3.1 percent. Excluding the two industries that appear in both small groups, the simple average advertising-to-sales ratios are 7.2 for the high advertisers and 1.36 for those thought to have economies of scale in advertising.

So it seems inadmissible to argue from these data that the advantages of size work against smaller firms (and presumably consumers) because scale economies in advertising "force" small firms to advertise more to overcome their disadvantage. And it is even less accurate to hold at the same time that the losses to heavy advertising show up where economies of scale in advertising exist. Comanor and Wilson's

---

[24]Comanor and Wilson, *Advertising and Market Power,* p. 211.
[25]Ibid., p. 198.

data show this to be true of two but untrue for six of the eight industries selected by their analysis. The whole demonstration boils down to two industries, drugs and perfumes. Only these two have both high advertising-to-sales ratios (9.9 percent and 15.3 percent) and high economies of scale to advertising by this test. Only these two industries meet the conditions illustrated in Figure 2 *and* the logic advanced in Comanor and Wilson's chapter 9.

Significantly, when a choice must be made, Comanor and Wilson go with the small group of eight with high advertising-to-sales ratios rather than with the group of seven. Perhaps this is because only there does room exist for more than trivial to modest price reductions should it prove possible to lower advertising expenditures at small cost to society or to consumers. But also if larger firms have *higher* advertising costs per unit of output, advertising loses much of its appeal as a low-cost barrier to entry by smaller firms. Rather it takes on the character of a high-cost defense against effective smaller rivals that squeezes the profits of the larger firms. If large firms that spend proportionally more on advertising are able to achieve some advantage, it is *despite* the lack of scale economies to advertising. If so, large firms that retain some advantage do so because they achieve greater economies in some other direction, such as lower production costs.

This advertising-as-defense-of-other-advantage argument is considerably weaker than the scale-economy-in-advertising argument because capital markets are thought to be more receptive to proposals to lower production cost than they are to finance advertising campaigns to expand markets. However, one must wonder why businesspeople and financiers should overlook any promising opportunity.

Which Measurement of Advertising Intensity? Comanor and Wilson use advertising-to-sales ratios to determine advertising intensity. They could have used absolute advertising volume per firm. The choice appears to have been made according to an often used econometric criterion: ". . . the advertising:sales ratio is a slightly stronger variable than the absolute volume of advertising per firm."[26] Presumably this means the advertising-to-sales ratio results in a higher R^2 than other variables in regressions run by the authors. The convention for choosing between two possible variables for inclusion on the basis of maximizing R^2 is valid only for cases where the researcher has equally valid theoretical reasons for accepting either definition.

There is a stronger case to be made in favor of the absolute volume of advertising as a barrier to entry as compared with advertising relative to sales. Increasing returns to scale of advertising seems clearly

---

[26]Ibid., p. 115.

more appropriately based on absolute levels of advertising than on the ratio of advertising to sales because the ratio of setup to running costs, quantity discounts, and the like are related to absolute amounts taken. So in this case, the use of the absolute level of advertising per firm is indicated by theory. The choice of the advertising-to-sales ratio makes it difficult to interpret later results, particularly the identification of those industries said to have excessive advertising. The surprising exclusion of motor vehicles, tires and tubes, radio, TV, and phonographs, and (marginally) cigarettes from the ranks of the heavy advertisers may not have occurred with absolute values. However, since differences among absolute levels were tested, there is a presumption against the likelihood that the final results would be significantly altered. Also the potential for significant price reduction diminishes as the advertising-to-sales ratio shrinks.

How Much Advertising Is Excessive? Excess advertising is found for only eight or eleven of the forty-one industries studied: eight if the cutoff advertising-to-sales ratio is 5 percent, eleven if it is 4 percent. Yet the amount of excess advertising by these industries is measured by comparing the actual level in the offending industry, not with the 4 percent or 5 percent "maximum values of competitive levels" chosen by Comanor and Wilson but with "the *mean* ratio for industries *below* the critical level."[27]

Accepting Comanor and Wilson's rule of 4 percent or 5 percent as the critical value of excessive advertising, an alternative and more reasonable method of calculating the costs of advertising drastically lowers the amount. For example, using cigarettes (4.8 percent advertising-to-sales ratio) and wines (5.2 percent ratio), compare the method of this study with Comanor and Wilson's. If 5.0 percent is used as the threshold level of excessive advertising, tobacco contributes nothing to the excessive costs of advertising. Following Comanor and Wilson's procedures, the amount of excessive advertising in the wine industry will depend on the average of advertising-to-sales ratios of all industries below the 5 percent critical level, which turns out to be 2.0 percent. According to Comanor and Wilson, this 2 percent (not 5 percent) is the benchmark above which the amount of advertising is to be considered excessive in the wine industry. Subtracting 2.0 from 5.2 obtains a 3.2 percent excessive advertising-to-sales ratio. Multiplying this by the level of sales gives the dollar amount of excess advertising. Note that cigarettes, with only a slightly smaller advertising-to-sales ratio, has no excess advertising by this test.

---

[27]Ibid., p. 242 (italics added).

Instead of subtracting the mean of all industries with ratios below the critical level, estimate the amount of advertising termed excessive by subtracting the critical level, 5 percent, rather than the truncated average level, 2 percent, from the actual amount. In the previous example of cigarettes and wine, cigarettes would continue to have no excess advertising but, using the 5 percent level, wines would have only 0.2 percent excessive advertising. Tables 4 and 5 show the approximate reduction in the excessive costs of advertising using alternative cutoffs.

While estimation of the dollar costs of excess advertising involves the necessity of knowing the actual sales levels (information not given in the book), it seems such a recalculation would lower Comanor and Wilson's estimate of the amount of excessive advertising by approximately 50 percent. Since the price-cost margin is calculated using the estimates of excess advertising, Comanor and Wilson's estimates of monopoly price and welfare loss are also subject to a downward revision.

Is Advertising an Expense or a Capital Asset? Comanor and Wilson's earlier work was criticized by Lester G. Telser for treating annual advertising as an expense rather than a short-term asset having more permanent value.[28] The effect of this in most cases would be to understate the equity of the firm, thus biasing profits upward. Since the effect is likely to be most pronounced for large amounts of advertising, a spurious positive correlation would be found between advertising and profit rates.

Comanor and Wilson reply to this criticism by devoting chapter 8 of their book to an investigation of the investment aspects of advertising. Their work is both theoretical and empirical, involving the estimation of "goodwill stocks" for the industry created by advertising. This is an attempt to determine the amount of advertising properly classified as investment. From this information they correct their rates of return and reestimate, via their regressions, the relationship between profits and advertising. They continue to find the effect of advertising to be positive and significant and conclude that it makes little or no difference whether advertising is treated as an investment or as a current expense ("expensed").

Their methods of estimating goodwill stocks, critical to this conclusion, are not persuasive. The essential point in their argument is

---

[28]Comanor and Wilson refer explicitly to Lester G. Telser, "Advertising and the Advantages of Size," *American Economic Review*, vol. 59 (May 1969), pp. 121–23; and Leonard W. Weiss, "Advertising, Profits, and Corporate Taxes," *Review of Economic Statistics*, vol. 51 (November 1969), pp. 421–29.

Table 4
Reduction in Excessive Advertising
Using a 5 Percent Critical Level

Industry	Advertising-Sales Ratio	Amount Excessive by Comanor and Wilson[a]	Amount Excessive Using 5 Percent[b]	Percent Change
Soft drinks	6.2%	4.2%	1.2%	−71%
Malt liquors	6.8	4.8	1.8	−62
Wines	5.2	3.2	0.2	−94
Cereals	10.3	8.3	5.3	−36
Drugs	9.9	7.9	4.9	−38
Soaps	9.2	7.2	4.2	−42
Perfumes	15.3	13.3	10.3	−23
Clocks and watches	5.6	3.6	0.6	−83
			Average reduction	56%

[a] This is found by subtracting 2.0, the mean ratio for all industries with advertising-sales ratios below 4 percent, from the actual advertising-sales ratios.
[b] This is found by subtracting the critical value (5.0 percent) from the actual level.
Source: Comanor and Wilson, *Advertising and Market Power,* table 6.A.2, pp. 134–35.

Table 5
Reduction in Excessive Advertising
Using a 4 Percent Critical Level

Industry	Advertising-Sales Ratio	Amount Excessive by Comanor and Wilson[a]	Amount Excessive Using 4 Percent[b]	Percent Change
Soft drinks	6.2%	4.4%	2.2%	−50%
Malt liquors	6.8	5.0	2.8	−44
Wines	5.2	3.4	1.2	−65
Cereals	10.3	8.5	6.3	−26
Cigarettes	4.8	3.0	0.8	−73
Drugs	9.9	8.1	5.9	−27
Soaps	9.2	7.4	5.2	−30
Perfumes	15.3	13.5	11.3	−16
Hand tools	4.2	2.4	0.2	−92
Clocks and watches	5.6	3.8	1.6	−58
Costume jewelry	4.0	2.2	0	−100
			Average reduction	53%

[a] This is found by subtracting 1.8, the mean ratio for all industries with advertising-sales ratios below 4 percent, from the actual advertising-sales ratios.
[b] This is found by subtracting the critical value (4.0 percent) from the actual level.
Source: Comanor and Wilson, *Advertising and Market Power,* table 6.A.2, pp. 134–35.

that while advertising adds asset values to one firm by building customer acceptance, it does so by reducing the asset values of competing firms' advertising by taking customers from them. From a social point of view, they argue, only the net increase in asset values for the industry as a whole should be counted, and if this is done, they say, advertising adds little to assets, so the rate of return is properly related to the smaller amount of socially useful assets.

This assertion about the method of correcting rates of return bears closer examination. Almost any effective competitive action taken by a firm can be expected to lower the asset values of its competitors. Thus, purchasing or building a capital asset that expands the capacity of a specific industry must be expected to reduce the value of similar capital held by others. Yet no adjustment to obtain net industry capital value is made when one firm adds to capacity. Indeed, if a reduction of the value of the rivals' assets occurs, it is likely to be viewed as socially desirable in any industry that had been enjoying a monopoly return. There is no obvious reason why advertising should be treated differently. There is no clear dividing line between expenditures to increase production and those that increase sales. Larger capacity or improved quality enhance availability and sales appeal, perhaps more than information and persuasion. Yet physical output is waste unless potential consumers learn of the wants it can assuage, its availability, and the like. All these complementary expenditures that are expected to improve sales in the future are subject to depreciation and obsolescence because of the action of rivals in the market. If competition is desirable, this is inevitable.

Two aspects of this controversy can be evaluated statistically. One is the extent to which advertising merely shifts customers from one firm to another (that is, is "wasted" in rivalry), and the other is the effect on profit rates among industries when advertising is thought of as creating capital values.

Comanor and Wilson argue that excessive advertising is more "rivalrous" than price cuts, that is, merely shifts customers among firms without expanding the total demand for the industry as a whole. This proposition can be tested by referring to their own work.[29] They calculate elasticities relating industry output alternatively to advertising, income, and price (both long and short run) for thirty-six of the forty-one consumer goods manufacturing industries. So it is possible to use their data to see if industries characterized by heavy advertising merely shift consumers among rivals. If it does, the *industry* responsiveness to advertising will be zero. This is not the case.

---

[29]Comanor and Wilson, *Advertising and Market Power*, pp. 89–90.

Three groups of industries are of interest: the group of eight with high advertising-to-sales ratios; the group of seven, found to have economies of scale in advertising, and the remaining twenty-three industries. The last two columns of Table 3 present the data for the three groupings. As already noted, two industries, drugs and perfumes, are in both groups. Simple averages for the two groups and the remaining twenty-three industries are given in the bottom four lines. Considerable variation exists among computed elasticities showing the responsiveness of sales to advertising within every group, but the average responsiveness of total industry demand to total industry advertising is rather high for each of the three groupings. In fact, the response of sales to advertising is *greatest* for the eight industries where advertising-to-sales ratios are the highest. This is the reverse of expectation if advertising is rivalrous where advertising-to-sales ratios are high. Instead, advertising seems to expand industry sales and, inferentially, expand utility more than in other industries. But the differences are rather small, so there seems to be little statistical basis for separating the industries with high advertising-to-sales ratios from the others, and certainly no basis for arguing that advertising in those industries is less valuable than in the other industries. Paradoxically, Comanor and Wilson stress the superior reliability of advertising in expanding *industry* sales, as compared with price reductions. These results strongly support the argument that advertising, no less than price cuts, contributes to socially useful values in industry generally and specifically in those industries displaying high advertising-to-sales ratios.

The inclusion of such values among assets virtually wipes out the high rates of profit Comanor and Wilson associate with heavy advertising. Harry Bloch and Robert Ayanian in separate studies using different techniques to estimate the investment effects of advertising reach this conclusion.[30] Bloch investigates profit rates and advertising for forty firms for the period 1950–1953, the period immediately preceding that covered by Comanor and Wilson (1954–1957). Bloch seeks an accurate measure of the firm's advertising capital by examining the difference between book and market value of the firm's stock. He argues that inappropriate accounting treatment of advertising for tax purposes will be reflected in the market value of the firm's stock. Using varying depreciation rates, he runs regressions on the differences between market and book value as the independent variable and

---

[30]Harry Bloch, "Advertising and Profitability: A Reappraisal," *Journal of Political Economy*, vol. 82, part 1 (March/April 1974), pp. 267–86; Robert Ayanian, "Advertising and Rates of Return," *Journal of Law and Economics*, vol. 18, no. 2 (October 1975), pp. 479–506. For a discussion of Bloch and Ayanian along with additional material on the correction of rates of return, see Kenneth W. Clarkson, *Intangible Capital and Rates of Return* (Washington, D.C.: American Enterprise Institute, 1977).

chooses the depreciation rate for advertising that maximizes R^2. This depreciation rate turns out to be 5 percent, which, when applied to the rates of return in forty firms, results in no relationship between profits and advertising. In his conclusion Bloch notes:

> The evidence presented above indicates that a strong positive relationship between measured profit rates and advertising intensity disappears when the profit rates are adjusted to correct for the expensing of advertising. Thus, the view that a positive relationship between measured profit rates and advertising intensity indicates the need for corrective policy toward advertising seems unwarranted.[31]

One may object to Bloch's procedure on the ground that some rate is bound to equalize these two values. A more cogent objection to Bloch's procedure has to do with the source of the profits "explained" by investment in advertising. It does not distinguish between socially undesirable "monopoly" returns hypothesized by critics of advertising and socially desirable "competitive" returns hypothesized by its proponents. Still, 5 percent is a low depreciation rate on advertising investment.

Robert Ayanian uses still another methodological approach in investigating this same issue. An important distinction between Ayanian's estimation procedure and the others is his attempt to find a separate depreciation rate for each industry. This is reasonable because advertising for different products at different stages of product life must be expected to have different depreciation rates. Although Ayanian ignores everything other than varying rates of depreciation across industries, his approach represents an improvement over standard depreciation rates for advertising across a whole economy.

Ayanian proceeds in an imaginative way. He finds firms with approximately equal sales-to-asset ratios but with divergent advertising growth rates. First he compares the correlation between advertising intensity and profit rates determined in the usual way. Then he compares the correlation calculated on a larger asset base, which includes some capital values created by advertising. The initial calculation yields essentially the relationship found by Comanor and Wilson. The second one does not. His procedure for the second calculation is to assume a geometric depreciation pattern and to calculate from this the one depreciation rate consistent with the particular proportionality between sales-to-asset ratios of divergent advertising growth rates. When this is done, a specific rate and capital value of advertising is found for six industries on the basis of data from thirty-nine firms for

---

[31]Bloch, "Advertising and Profitability," p. 283.

the period 1959–1965. These industries—autos, cosmetics, drugs, electrical products, foods (including separate data on cereals)—bear some resemblance to the list of heavy advertisers identified by Comanor and Wilson and other critics of advertising.

Ayanian finds depreciation rates differing substantially, from about 5 percent a year for autos to almost 40 percent for foods. After estimating depreciation rates, he corrects the accounting rates of return for these thirty-nine firms and finds that the relationship between advertising intensity and profitability falls apart when corrected profit rates are used. The t-statistic on the advertising variable falls from a significant 3.445 to 0.884 and R^2, from 0.243 to 0.021.

Ayanian tests his corrections to determine how much of the variation in accounting rates of return can be explained by the usual practice of treating advertising as an expense rather than as a capital asset. By a simple test, he obtains a result that over 65 percent of the variation can be explained in this way. Ayanian therefore concludes:

> The results of this paper are completely at odds with the "barriers to entry" view of advertising. Over a wide range of advertising intensity and diverse products there appears to be no systematic relationship between advertising and profitability—once the asset nature of advertising is taken into account. As one might have suspected, freedom of speech is compatible with competition.[32]

The differences in results among Comanor and Wilson, Bloch, and Ayanian are evident in Table 6. It presents the amount of correction each obtains by treating advertising as an investment in the industries included in two or more studies. A degree of caution is warranted. The table refers to different time periods (Bloch's 1950–1953; Comanor and Wilson's 1954–1957; and Ayanian's 1968), so direct comparisons may be infeasible. Also Ayanian and Bloch measure profit rates originating by firm. These have been aggregated into industry rates for compatibility with Comanor and Wilson's. Since only an unweighted sample of the largest firms in the aggregation is given, some systematic bias in the industry profits may be present. Differences in the amount of adjustment made by each author are obvious. In the thirty-nine firms examined by Ayanian, the average firm profit rate fell from 14.85 percent to 11.32 percent, a downward adjustment of 23.8 percent. Similarly, Bloch's adjustment on forty firms is a downward adjustment from 10.23 percent to 8.36 percent, a decline of 18.3 percent. On the other hand, Comanor and Wilson's adjustment is of no significance, being slightly *upward* in two cases. The simple average of their adjustments

---

[32] Ayanian, "Advertising and Rates of Return," p. 506.

Table 6

Corrections for Investment Aspects of Advertising

COMANOR AND WILSON

Industry	Profit Rate	Adjusted Profit Rate
Distilled liquors	5.007%	4.960%
Meat	4.644	4.644
Dairy products	7.936	7.909
Canning	6.428	6.522
Cereals	14.811	13.796
Bakery products	9.279	9.295
Drugs	13.981	13.935
Soaps	11.653	11.554
Perfumes	13.534	13.414
Tires and tubes	10.236	10.236
Electrical appliances	10.523	10.523
Radio, TV, phonograph	8.789	8.409
Motor vehicles	15.461	15.461

AYANIAN

Industry	Depreciation Rate	Profit Rate	Adjusted Profit Rate
Autos	0.051/year	14.83%	11.08%
Cosmetics	0.128	19.99	11.68
Electrical	0.124	13.76	11.46
Foods	0.368	12.70	10.74
—cereals	0.368	14.45	11.19
Tires	0.147	11.08	10.27
Drugs	0.087	16.45	12.59

BLOCH

Industry	Profit Rate	Adjusted Profit Rate
Distilled liquors	10.1%	8.1%
Dairy products	11.0	9.2
Soft drinks	12.9	9.2
Malt beverages	12.1	10.3
Canning and processing	10.5	8.2
Meat	6.9	6.0
Baking	11.5	9.3
Cereals	13.9	8.8

Sources: Comanor and Wilson, *Advertising and Market Power,* table 8.2, pp. 188–89. This is their adjustment b_2. See pp. 180–93 for its derivation. Ayanian, "Advertising and Rates of Return," table 6, p. 499. All industry profit rates are unweighted averages of firm profit rates. Depreciation rates are from table I, p. 494. Bloch, "Advertising and Profitability," table A1, p. 285. Bloch's estimate P_2, reported net income after taxes divided by reported net worth and the corresponding adjusted profit rate, is used here.

for the industries that roughly correspond to the six of Ayanian is about one percent downward.[33]

Comanor and Wilson's findings are sensitive to their method of correcting profit rates for the asset values advertising creates. Since, counter to their expectations, their data reveal a greater industrywide responsiveness to advertising where advertising intensity is high, and evidently undervalue the capital value of advertising, their case against excess advertising is weak.

Unfortunately, Ayanian's work does not escape the possibility that the capital values created by advertising are founded on monopoly rather than on competition. Profit-maximizing monopoly no less than competition will equalize returns on every margin. The notion that advertising builds values that last for several years is a reasonable one, and, if so, the argument becomes one of deciding whether the value is excessive in the particular industry. Ayanian's analysis certainly supports the probability that rate of return is competitive.

Advertising and Elasticities. Advertising may still be condemned if it creates asset values by making demand curves less elastic, as is expected in some a priori theorizing. If it did this, it might be possible to charge a higher price without losing many sales. The hypothesis that associates high advertising-to-sales ratios with relatively inelastic demand can again be tested against data provided by Comanor and Wilson. The last column of Table 3 summarizes their data. Seven of the eight industries with advertising-to-sales ratios over 5 percent are found to have negatively sloped demand curves, the exception being perfumes, which Comanor and Wilson believe to be a Veblen-good, that is, one consumers believe to be worth more *because* it is higher priced. (But why is the price not raised more?) The industries with negative slopes have elasticities ranging from -0.784 to -9.802 with an unweighted average (even excluding the extreme -9.802) of -1.392. This compares to a range of 0.0 to -1.695 (the latter for drugs, which is also among the eight) for the group of seven having possible economies of scale in advertising. The average for the remaining twenty-three industries with downward sloping curves for which long-run elasticities are computed is -0.846.

Consequently, it seems likely that the industries characterized by high advertising intensity as indicated by high advertising-to-sales ratios are also characterized by more elastic demand curves than the others. This supports, albeit weakly, the notion that advertising intensity is a sign of greater competition rather than less. It is strong evi-

---

[33]Comanor and Wilson's conclusions are given in *Advertising and Market Power*, pp. 191–93.

dence against both the Robinsonian view that advertising creates a less elastic demand curve and the Chamberlinian belief that greater advertising intensity will be found in industries where the demand curve is less elastic. It is consistent with the previously discussed elasticities of sales to advertising intensity. Industry sales in industries characterized by high advertising-to-sales ratios are found to be more responsive than the others, both to changes in advertising intensity and to price changes. This supports the competitive rather than the monopolistic presumption about the effect of advertising.

Costs of Suboptimal Capacity. The second large social cost of elasticity obtained by Comanor and Wilson is attributable to smaller firms operating at high costs while sheltered by high price-cost margins determined and maintained by larger firms. Comanor and Wilson estimate this cost for all forty-one industries, although it appears out of place to include the thirty-three industries found not to engage in excessive advertising. In those industries, any social cost must be attributed to other causes. The amount of loss attributed to nonexcessive advertising is pulled out and compared to the heavy advertisers in Table 2 and is discussed in that part of this chapter.

Comanor and Wilson's estimates of costs of suboptimal capacity are obtained from equations predicting the differences in profits from operating above or below a calculated minimum efficient plant size *(MES)*. They investigate two candidates for determining the minimum efficient plant size. One is the survival technique developed by Leonard W. Weiss from a model innovated by George J. Stigler. The other is based on the costs of the average-sized plant using the largest plants accounting for 50 percent of industry output. To decide which proxy variable to use, Comanor and Wilson compare the results from each of the two methods with results obtained by Joe S. Bain. Estimates based on the survival technique showed a correlation of 0.66, while the use of size distribution of plants resulted in a correlation of 0.86. Thus, using Bain's work as a benchmark, they choose the latter technique of determining *MES*.[34]

The estimate of higher costs to firms is derived from the differential costs of plants by a formula that, basically, attributes a lower profit to firms whose size is smaller than the smallest efficient-sized plant in its particular industry. The estimation procedure is worked out in detail in Comanor and Wilson's chapter 6. The variables are: two measures of advertising intensity, the concentration ratio, absolute capital requirements, economies of scale, growth of demand, and a

---

[34]Ibid., pp. 112–13.

local market dummy. The technique of relating these variables to profit rates largely avoids an overly restricted view of potential scale economies that, from an economic view, must encompass the net effect of all types of costs. Although this technique is continued, the formula used in the final chapter to calculate welfare loss to excessive cost by small firms uses the following simple formula, based on a previously obtained regression investigation of the profit rate differences between firms above and below the estimated minimum efficient scale *(MES)*.[35]

$$PD = -0.0315 \ln \frac{SL2}{MES} \tag{1}$$

PD = profit rate difference
SL2 = mean sales for firms below *MES*
MES = estimated minimum efficient scale of plant

Neither this nor any other of a number of different tested equations works particularly well.

Since the corporate income tax rate is about 50 percent, the profit differential is doubled to make it correspond to before-tax profits. Multiplying this first by the equity-to-sales ratio and then by sales of the firms below *MES* gives a dollar value of the cost of operating a firm that is below the minimum efficient size for a plant. For example, suppose the calculation shows 3 percent lower profit rate for plants operating below *MES*. Multiplying by two gives a 6 percent profit difference before taxes. If the smaller firms have a 10 percent equity-to-sales ratio and a $100 million sales figure, the dollar loss would be

$.06 \times .10 \times 100,000,000 = \$60,000$

Comanor and Wilson note that sales include firms below $500,000 asset size. This was used as a cutoff point earlier when the regression results built into equation (1) were obtained. They report profit rates to firms below $500,000 asset size to be highly volatile, possibly introducing a systematic bias into the estimate of costs of suboptimal capacity.[36] Other difficulties cast doubt on the size and even the existence of this loss. Three of the forty-one industries found all smaller firms below the $500,000 cutoff, necessitating a horseback estimate. More importantly, twelve of the forty-one industries were excluded from many of these calculations because the hypothesized positive relationship between firm size and profits did not hold. Instead, the smaller firms were found to have the lower costs.[37] These industries had somewhat lower advertising-to-sales ratios, while big firm plants had somewhat higher

---

[35] Ibid., p. 242, n. 3.
[36] Ibid., p. 222.
[37] Ibid., p. 228.

ratios relative to their industry than the average of the included twenty-nine industries. These industries were included in the final calculations, but the effect of this is not evident.

Even if the relationships among firm size, plant size, and profits were clearly valid, the conclusions implied would be ambiguous. The diversity of products included in the conglomerate industries makes it possible for efficient smaller firms to appear inefficient because the efficient size of plant is determined from other noncompeting products and larger submarkets within the too broad industry category. The same diversity makes for different profit rates, each appropriate to competitive conditions within its intra-industry sector. Differences in composition within the forty-one industries can be relatively stable and produce differences like those found in the present study that meet the usual tests for statistical significance.

Use of data for products that compete directly in the same market avoids this problem. Very little such data exist, but Jean-Jacques Lambin has made a study of a number of brands of sixteen commodities in Europe. The products include soft drinks, electric shavers, gasoline, television sets, cigarettes, deodorants, detergents, and coffee. His study does not include firm or industry profits among its variables, but it does focus on advertising as a barrier to entry, market power, market conduct, market performance, and ability to differentiate products (called by Lambin "advertising" and "consumer buying behavior"). In his summary table 7.2, entitled "The Advertising Controversy Revisited," many of his conclusions begin "Yes, but." For example, with regard to brand loyalty as a barrier to entry, he finds that yes, it exists, but "In our sample, no positive or statistically significant relationship is observed between brand inertia rates and various measures of brand advertising intensity."[38] He finds that advertising contributes to *active* rivalry; is complementary to other types of rivalry, such as technological wars and price cutting; and is not related to concentration, although smaller firms need to spend more per unit of sales because of a "threshold" effect.[39]

None of this directly contradicts the argument that society may have to bear some burdens because some firms are inefficiently undersize. It does so indirectly because it finds advertising to be much more of an aid to competition than to monopoly, a condition that reveals advertising to be most often a device that brings quicker victory to the more efficient producer engaged in particular battles in the incessant "technological war."

---

[38]Lambin, *Advertising, Competition, and Market Conduct*, p. 160.
[39]Ibid., pp. 166–67.

Role of the Corporation Income Tax. The size of the loss to inefficient production by too small firms is doubled by Comanor and Wilson because the loss was calculated from a profit differential and the corporation income tax takes approximately half of corporate income. This doubling of the loss is not justified. If one accepts the theory that the corporation pays the tax, so that it has no effect on consumer prices, the tax paid by the larger corporations does not affect price and cannot raise the cost that smaller firms can live with. Nor would the smaller firms change their resource use or sales because of the tax. If payment of the corporate income tax does not affect resource allocation, it is hard to see how it can impose a social loss or a loss to consumers. In that case, abolition of the corporation tax would transfer more of the tax burden of government to others, presumably the consumer (assuming an unchanged level of government expenditure), but it would be a transfer and not a social cost.

Another, and perhaps more reasonable, theory of the incidence of the corporation income tax is that it is eventually passed on to the consumers in one form or another. Suppose that it is passed on directly in price. Now the price set by the larger firms will include the corporation income tax and will allow small firms to operate under lessened competitive pressure if it happens that they pay little or no tax because their inefficient or higher cost operations keep their costs up. The difference in tax paid may even fully account for the difference in profits. The difference does measure how much higher costs are in the smaller firms, and it is not entirely unreasonable to suppose that larger firms could have produced the output of the smaller ones with a smaller use of resources. But this provides no reason to double the difference. The tax does not confer an additional advantage to the larger firms, assuming for the sake of the argument that they are more profitable.

Harberger-type Deadweight Welfare Loss. The smallest of the calculated welfare losses to society ironically requires the greatest amount of explanation. The loss is obtained for each industry separately by the use of the equation

$$AL_{(i)} = \tfrac{1}{2}(M_{(i)} + CSO_{(i)} + X_{(i)})^2 \, (-ES_{(i)})S_{(i)} \qquad (2)$$

where AL is the absolute value of the allocative efficiency loss in a particular industry i, M is the before-tax excess profit margin on its sales, CSO is the cost of suboptimal capacity in that industry, X is the excess advertising cost expressed as a ratio to industry sales, $-ES$ is the industry's short-run price elasticity of demand, and S is the total sales of the industry. The losses for each industry are summed to get a figure for the forty-one industries examined.[40]

The logic of this approach is as follows. The difference between the existing ("monopoly") price and the competitive price ("monopoly markup") is estimated as the percent of industry sales that goes to excess profits (M), higher average industry costs (CSO), and excess advertising expense (X), each spread over the whole value of sales of the industry. The size of the loss also depends upon how much more would have been purchased if the price had been at the lower (competitive) level. This is estimated from the demand elasticity. If the demand elasticity is -1.0, a 1 percent lower price results in a 1 percent increase in sales; if elasticity is -2.0, sales will expand 2 percent. One rather neat way to make this calculation, and the one used here, is, in a sense, to assume that the elasticity is initially -1.0 so one can simply square the monopoly markup; then multiply the result by the actual elasticity of demand. This produces a number with everything stated in terms of the percent of sales. To get a dollar amount it is necessary, therefore, to multiply it by the dollar value of sales, S. The resulting number is, however, approximately twice the size of loss because the value of additional units of the good declines as more become available. (Were this not so, the demand curve would be flat, with the implication that the consumer would be happier if all the world's resources were devoted to expanding the output of any particular monopolized industry!)

The elasticity of demand tells us how rapidly the value of additional units falls. A straight line between the observed (monopoly) quantity and price and the calculated (competitive) price and quantity bisects the rectangle found when the monopoly markup was squared and multiplied by the price elasticity of demand. Look again at Figure 2 to visualize these relationships that result in area L.

This formula produces surprisingly small welfare losses. The primary reason for this is that people easily forget the basic observational truth that resources not used in one industry are used in others. There is a welfare loss due to misallocation only to the extent that the resources would have produced things of greater value in the "monopolized" industry than they actually produced where they were. The cost per unit of production—excluding excessive advertising expenses, the higher costs of suboptimal firms, and the excess profits—measures how much had to be paid to attract and hold cur-

---

[40]Comanor and Wilson, *Advertising and Market Power*, p. 243. The use of short-run elasticity reduces the estimate of deadweight welfare loss somewhat because long-run elasticities are larger. Tables 3 and 8 present the long-run elasticities that are more favorable to their case.

rently employed resources in the "monopolized" industry, and, it is assumed, is the amount that would have to be paid per unit of output to attract more resources into it. If the industry is large, this is probably an underestimate of the cost of expanding output to the estimated competitive amount, and if it is, the size of the welfare loss L in Figure 2 is exaggerated.

It may be helpful to run through a numerical calculation. Suppose the monopoly markup is estimated at 15 percent of sales, the price elasticity of demand at −2.0, and industry sales at $1,000. Square .15 to get .0225 and multiply by elasticity to find .045. (The minus in the formula cancels the minus in the value.) Multiplying by industry sales yields $45.00, half of which, $22.50, is a welfare loss. This is 2.25 percent of industry sales, which is very large when compared to the losses that are usually found. It is large because the markup is high and because the elasticity is also high. Comanor and Wilson state the percentage loss in terms of value added. This subtracts from sales the value of supplies purchased from other firms and raises the percentage figure. The $140 million loss is given as thirty-one hundredths of one percent of value added by Comanor and Wilson.

In view of the small loss, only 9.1 percent of the social loss and 5.4 percent of the total loss to consumers reported by Comanor and Wilson, it may not be worthwhile to subject this estimate to close examination. If it is accurate, and if it were completely removed without cost, consumers would gain only three-tenths of 1 percent of value added by these industries; less than three-hundredths of 1 percent of personal consumption expenditures. Nevertheless, this figure is grossly exaggerated.

First, anything that increases the monopoly markup increases the loss by the square of the increase. It has already been shown that the amount of advertising that can properly be termed excessive, if there is any, is much less than the amount displayed by Comanor and Wilson. This study has argued that the loss assigned to suboptimal capacity is excessive and surely should not be doubled because of the corporate income tax. This brings us to the two remaining terms in the equation that affect the asserted price markup, the size of excess profits and the price elasticities of demand.

Comanor and Wilson calculate excessive profits for each industry by comparing actual profits for the industry as a whole with competitive profits obtained with the equation

$$P = aA + bACR + cLD + dG \tag{3}$$

where P is competitive profit, A is the advertising-to-sales ratio set alternatively at 4 percent and 5 percent, ACR is the absolute capital requirement set at the median amount for all forty-one industries. *LD* is the local market dummy set at zero, and *G* is the growth rate set for each industry at its own rate. The lower the calculated competitive profit *P*, the greater the "excess" profits.[41] This procedure makes no direct use of the estimated excess costs of advertising, suboptimal capacity, or monopoly profits, but equation (3) is designed to capture these influences, and it can be assumed that it does.

The excess profit found in this way is again essentially doubled to get the amount prices are said to be inflated by profits on the assumption that half the profits earned are siphoned off by the federal corporation income tax. This step clearly reveals the theory of tax incidence embraced by Comanor and Wilson. It is seen as directly raising prices to consumers by the amount of the tax. (Consistent with this view, the $1,070 million monopoly transfer from consumers to business, assuming a 5 percent advertising-to-sales ratio, recorded by Comanor and Wilson's table 11.1, is not doubled because after-tax profits is all that business retains.[42] This is discussed further in the next section.)

Doubling the excess profit for purposes of estimating what the competitive price would be in the absence of monopoly probably inflates the markup above that illustrated in Figure 2. The effect of doubling profits can be discovered if we can rely on the estimated losses by category given in Comanor and Wilson's tables 11.1 and 11.2 and summarized in this study's Table 2. Excess profits are recorded as $1,070 million for all firms, whether or not they are heavy advertisers, assuming a 5 percent critical advertising-to-sales ratio. Total expenses plus profits that assertedly raise prices to consumers are given as $2,562 million. Doubling profits increases the estimated monopoly markup 41.7 percent ($1,070/$2,562) and the total share of profits in the markup to 58.9 percent ($2,140/$3,632). Curiously, the effect of profits, even when doubled, is much smaller for industries labeled excessive advertisers. Only 27.8 percent of the price increase is due to high profits, primarily because of the heavy weight of advertising expense in the total.

The second element determining the size of the Harberger-type deadweight loss is the elasticity of demand. Comanor and Wilson estimate demand elasticities for all forty-one industries in their chapter 5. These are a welcome addition to the literature.[43] The values found

---

[41]This cannot come from Table 7.1, equation (2) as referenced by Comanor and Wilson (p. 242, n. 4). It seems to come from Table 6.4, equation (5), p. 119.

[42]Ibid., pp. 242–43.

[43]I displayed all the demand elasticities I could find in "On Monopoly Welfare Losses" cited earlier. Comanor and Wilson's estimates came to my attention after my paper was published.

are consistent with those of other investigators and, being small, account for the small size of the estimated deadweight loss. They employ a generalized Koyck-type model similar to that used by Houthakker-Taylor to estimate short-run and long-run elasticities for price, income, and advertising. On occasions when their model does not seem to obtain reasonable results, Comanor and Wilson use a model they refer to as the flow-adjustment model. Here, change in consumption depends on the difference between desired and actual consumption. Although some technical objections can be made, they are not important to the size of the welfare losses computed and in any case lead to problems interesting only to specialists in econometric theory.

How Large and How Damaging to Consumers Is the "Monopoly Transfer"? Table 2 noted the finding, damaging to Comanor and Wilson's conclusions, that something between 78 percent and 86 percent of excess profits received by manufacturers of consumer goods are garnered by firms not found by Comanor and Wilson to be excessive advertisers. Excessive profits are categorized as transfers, rather than social costs, because no inefficient use of resources is directly involved. The monopolizing agent gains all the consumer loses. In calculating the transfer, only the part of profits that are retained by the firms is classified as a transfer injurious to consumers. It amounts to $1,070 million of the $2,602 million total loss to consumers if the 5 percent advertising-to-sales ratio is used. Only $148 million of the monopoly transfer is attributed to excessive advertisers.

If the full before-tax profits raise prices to consumers, why should not the full tax be counted as a transfer? Possibly because it is considered a payment for government services that have a value equal to or greater than the tax cost to consumers. If so, a socially valuable function is performed, but the financing is still predominantly a transfer from the consumers of the high profit goods to other consumers who would otherwise have to pay higher taxes. (Parenthetically, one should observe the arbitrary exclusion of profit-takers from the ranks of "consumers" and the inclusion of everybody else.) Only the individual consumer's "fair share" of government taxes is part of the necessary costs of government that the consumers of high profit goods should pay. The rest, according to the logic of tax incidence apparently embraced by Comanor and Wilson, is a transfer from those who buy highly taxed goods to other consumers.

The treatment of government expenditures as socially functional and the remaining profits as a socially useless transfer must be questioned. Are all the profits called excess in this study without socially useful effects? Would our society work as effectively if they were absent? Probably not. The directive function of profits and losses, the placing of investment funds in the hands of the more perceptive entrepreneurs, and the incentives of large prizes that provoke energetic work by many who are not likely to be motivated by bureaucratic life styles—Schumpeter's creative destruction form of competition—may, as Schumpeter observed, have very large payoffs for consumers. The unexamined assumption that transfers to government collected via a corporation income tax is costless to consumers because the government functions are valuable, while above average profits received by business for whatever reason are costly to consumers because they are without socially useful function is, to say the least, one-sided. But it also reflects a popular view that makes analyses like these potentially effective in shaping legislation.

General Criticisms of Welfare Loss Calculations

This analysis of Comanor and Wilson's intensive investigation of the effect of advertising on social and consumer welfare has, thus far, accepted their analytical framework and only contested the size of the costs and losses. More fundamental matters, until now only hinted at, require explicit treatment. Table 7 repeats some data present in Table 2 for advertising-to-sales ratios of 5 percent and contrasts the average losses of heavy advertisers with the others. Except for the advertising outlays deemed excessive and necessarily attributed entirely to the heavy advertisers, there is little difference in the social loss or loss to consumer per industry studied. Leaving advertising out of the account, the loss per industry to suboptimal capacity and to monopoly transfer is clearly higher for the normal advertisers; the opposite difference in deadweight loss by no means compensates. The one thing that is clear is that the welfare losses of normal advertisers are not attributed to market power based on advertising. But since losses in those industries are, if anything, greater than those where advertising is excessive, a reasonable person must entertain a null and a counter hypothesis. Perhaps heavy advertising has nothing to do with welfare loss (the null hypothesis); or, since the losses to consumers other than the perhaps excessive advertising appear rather smaller where advertising is heavy, and much smaller overall if the loss attributed directly to "excess" advertising is left out of account, advertising or excess advertising is more accurately seen as a tool that breaks down monopoly otherwise established ambiguously on some unexplained basis. Either of these interpretations fits the Table 7 data better than the advertising-as-a-way-to-monopolize theory.

45

Table 7

Losses to Society and to Consumers: Heavy and Nonheavy Advertising Industries Compared

(millions of dollars)

Type of Loss	The 8 Heavy Advertisers	The Other 33	Average for the 8	Average for the 33	Average for all 41
Excess advertising	$656	$ 0	$ 82.0	$ 0	$16.0
Cost of suboptimal capacity	112	624	14.0	18.9	18.0
Deadweight loss	62	78	7.75	2.4	3.4
Monopoly transfer	148	922	18.5	27.9	26.1
Total	978	1624	122.25	49.2	63.5
Less advertising	322	1624	40.25	49.2	47.5

Source: Adapted from Table 2, cols. 3, 5.

The earlier discussion associated with Figure 2 accepted, provisionally, the notion that advertising does not shift the industry demand curve, but rather allows firms to set a higher price, and sell less, along an unchanged demand curve. This provisional acceptance is contrary to the implications of the data for advertising-to-sales ratios, elasticities of sales-to-advertising expenditures, and price elasticities of demand presented in Comanor and Wilson's table 5–8 and also in Lambin's findings for interrelationships among brands of narrowly defined consumer goods. Both find higher price elasticities where advertising-to-sales ratios are high and *industrywide* sales that are responsive to changes in advertising, all of them working as tools of competition and rivalry rather than monopoly or restriction.

If advertising, including heavy advertising, shifts the *industry* demand curve to the right, as the evidence indicates it does, it is far more likely to result in *gains*, not losses, for society and consumers. The source of gains is in the provision of all kinds of information at less cost to the consumer, including new ideas about what would be enjoyable. Geometrically, all gains are implicit in a shift of the demand curve, such as from D_0 to D_{A_1} in Figure 3. Average and marginal costs without heavy advertising are horizontal at C_0 and with heavy advertising are equal in amount to $C_{A_1}C_0BB_1$, illustrated by the descending line C_A.[44]

Note that price cuts from C_0 are not possible without losses to the

---

[44]In this case, advertising expense is assumed to be the same at every output.

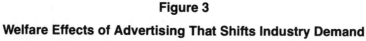

Figure 3

Welfare Effects of Advertising That Shifts Industry Demand

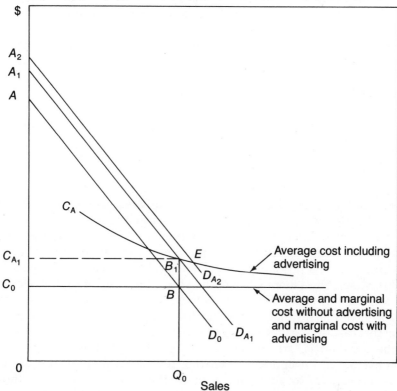

industry and that industrywide demand is shifted by advertising, eliminating any purely rivalrous advertising that merely shifts sales from one firm to another within the same industry. When advertising shifts the industry demand curve vertically to $A_1D_{A_1}$, so that the same quantity may be sold at the higher price C_{A_1} rather than C_0, there is neither a gain nor a loss to society or to the consumers in the case illustrated because the consumer surplus without heavy advertising, C_0BA, is exactly equal to consumer surplus with heavy advertising, $C_{A_1}B_1A_1$. In practice, either gains or losses can occur because the upward shift of the demand curve may also steepen or flatten it. Unfortunately, there is no way to discover the position of the demand curve at all levels of output. All the tests for welfare loss used by Comanor and Wilson, due to advertising and other causes as well, can only show losses, but there would be no losses in the case illustrated, and gains are possible or even likely.

Advertising that lowered the cost of search to consumers, or that gave some of them a new dimension, shows up in a higher curve. The fact that the same amount is sold at a higher price is prima facie evidence that one or both of these objectives have been served. Like any other cost, successful advertising raises the net values of consumers' utility. Profits may not have been increased. Any price along line C_A leaves profits the same as at B. But if increased advertising costing $C_0 B B_1 C_{A_1}$ shifts the demand curve to D_{A_2} and price E is obtained, consumer surplus is raised more than advertising costs (by the amount $A_2 A_1 B_1 E$) although the industry experiences no rise in profits. A large number of possible prices yield some profits without putting the consumer in as bad a position as he would be without advertising, even "excessive" advertising. In this connection it is important to recall that the industries said to advertise excessively display combinations of responses to advertising and price that are more favorable to the demand-shifting effect of advertising than are the other industries.

The foregoing suggests that the real arguments come down, once again, not to advertising, but to monopoly however achieved. The basic problem is that concentration seems to be based on real costs, conditions of a physical and technological type that make large scale firms sometimes more efficient than the others. Although the relevant markets may be immense, so that very large firms, such as Standard Oil of New Jersey, have rather small portions of the market (10 percent in that case), it is easy to believe that prices are set monopolistically. So the question is, are the economies of efficient scale passed on to consumers in lower prices, or are they retained as profits except as they are taxed away by government, or are they diverted to costs to those able to secure employment in the industry in excessive wages, salaries, and fringes? The answer to this question is beyond the scope of this book. An important paper by Sam Peltzman made the first comprehensive quantitative answer to the division between gain to consumers and monopoly price that I have seen. He, provisionally, finds the lion's share of the gain going to consumers.[45]

Summary

The literature on welfare loss has unresolved problems, especially with regard to the characterization of any profits that firms may make. Harberger regarded them as transfers without relevance to efficiency. Tullock, Posner, and others have seen in them incentives that result in

---

[45] Sam Peltzman, "The Gains and Losses from Industrial Concentration," *Journal of Law and Economics*, vol. 20, no. 2 (October 1977), pp. 229–63.

wasted resources. Comanor and Wilson have undertaken an arduous and intelligent path to seek out and measure such costs as may be related to advertising and add them to the very small welfare loss found by Harberger's procedures. This admirable empirical effort produces results that lead this study to support conclusions quite different from theirs. A close study of Comanor and Wilson's analysis of the relationship of market power to advertising weakens confidence that any such relationship exists. A number of decisions seem to have been made, each of which tends either to be neutral or to exaggerate the size of the calculated loss. One confusion into which it is easy to fall is a false identification of two sets of firms, both of which are vaguely referred to as a "small group." One is a group of seven that meets Comanor and Wilson's test for economies of scale in advertising, the other a group of eight classified as advertising excessively. Six of the eight with high advertising-to-sales ratios flunk the test for economies of scale in advertising and undermine Comanor and Wilson's theoretical basis for advertising as a barrier to entry and a source of monopoly power. Notwithstanding this, a very large part of the loss shown in the final tables turns out, on careful reading, not even to be asserted to be attributable to advertising.

Forty-three percent of the loss to society attributable to excessive advertising, two-thirds to three-quarters of the loss due to the industries engaging in it, is the advertising expenditure itself. The amount classified as excessive is approximately doubled by assuming that the industries characterized as having excess advertising are supposed to need no more than the average of the nonexcessive advertisers, rather than the maximum deemed competitive. The remaining loss to excessive advertising is reduced perhaps to zero, if, as seems reasonable, Ayanian and Bloch's analysis of advertising as a capital investment is accepted.

The social cost caused by firms operating with too small a capacity is calculated for industries that are "excessive" advertisers and also for the ones that are not. The variety of products and marketing conditions within each industry makes any determination of efficient scale controversial, but the fact that this cost is smaller per industry in industries said to advertise excessively suggests that this cost is not related to heavy advertising, or if it is, is related inversely. This finding contradicts the other theoretical argument for advertising as a barrier to entry. The production costs of smaller firms are not boosted in industries that advertise intensively. Moreover, doubling the size of the loss to allow for taxes seems to be an exaggeration, whether one believes that the corporation tax is passed on fully to the consumer or absorbed in profits. If it is added to prices, it is a transfer or a payment for valuable government services. Either way, it is not a social cost, and if it is not passed on, it is simply an exaggeration.

The deadweight loss is exaggerated by anything that increases the margin between calculated competitive price and actual price. The exaggeration of excess advertising expenditures and costs of suboptimal capacity both have this effect. So does any exaggeration of the "monopoly transfer," summarized next. For these reasons, even the small deadweight loss is overstated.

The principal point to be made with regard to the monopoly transfers calculated by Comanor and Wilson is that they are emphatically not associated with the heavy advertisers. Only 15 percent of such loss is attributed to them. The average monopoly transfer per industry that advertises intensively is about half the average for the other thirty-three industries that are not heavy advertisers. Monopoly transfer is the largest single source of loss to consumers reported by Comanor and Wilson, although it is not increased by them to adjust for the corporation income tax on the dubious ground that taxes on profits are beneficial to "consumers" while profits that remain under the control of the firms that produce them are not.

Finally, most of the base upon which the calculations under scrutiny rest is lost, if, as the econometric findings say should be done, the assumption is dropped that heavy advertising is strictly rivalrous and so does not save consumers costs, or, if advertising is recognized as lowering search costs and as increasing the satisfaction received from the products consumers purchase. If consumer surplus is raised by advertising, selling the same or fewer goods at higher prices may or may not involve a loss to consumers. But if, as the data tell us, output is positively correlated with advertising intensity, *and* higher prices are paid, the positive effect of heavy advertising on consumer satisfaction becomes a near certainty. In that case, little or none of the "excess" advertising can be properly counted as waste. Also, with larger industry sales, the relatively smaller-sized firms can be larger in absolute size, reducing whatever amount of suboptimal capacity as may exist. The welfare triangle is also greatly exaggerated by the hypothetical low competitive price found by subtracting the totality of these costs. Even the monopoly transfer takes on a different character, being more of a reward for discovering a cheaper way for consumers to discover specific ways to satisfy one or another of their latent, or until then more constrained, wants.

3

Remedies Proposed to Regulate the Effects of Advertising on Market Structure

In their final chapter, Comanor and Wilson do little more than hint at remedies to reduce the losses attributed directly and indirectly to excessive advertising. Their statements are diffidently put and qualified.[1] Nevertheless, these statements add up to an imposing array of bases for action that, if persuasive to the President, regulatory agencies, and courts, could extend regulatory actions considerably, and if persuasive to Congress, could have even greater impact. The remedies rest on a consumer protection theory of government regulation, which as summarized by William A. Jordan, implies

> that regulation will protect consumer interests by reducing prices until they equal marginal costs, by preventing discriminatory pricing, by improving service quality (at existing prices), by encouraging entry of firms that are more efficient or that offer more preferred price/product combinations, and by reducing industry profits to the market rate of return. These are essentially the results that would be expected under a competitive market structure and, indeed the results of such a market structure are frequently proposed as a regulatory model.[2]

This list is virtually the litany of benefits Comanor and Wilson associate with the regulation of advertising and other bases of monopoly. Their recommendations, or suggestions, for government action fall into two categories: eased conditions of entry for new firms and direct regulation of "natural oligopolies." Easier entry is favored if there is room for a large enough number of economically efficient firms to closely approximate the formal competitive structure. Only half the

---

[1]Comanor and Wilson, *Advertising and Market Power*, pp. 245–53.

[2]William A. Jordan, "Producer Protection, Prior Market Structure and the Effects of Government Regulation," *Journal of Law and Economics*, vol. 15 (April 1972), p. 152.

industries have potential for competition according to Comanor and Wilson's definitions and analysis. Direct regulation is a fall-back (or forward-thrust) position to which resort may be made in all the other cases. Both are seen as promoting competition in the technical sense of creating conditions where marginal social costs and marginal private costs are both equal to price in every industry.

Where feasible, improved entry conditions for new firms may be sought by establishing controls over the pricing of media services, with special reference to eliminating quantity discounts for TV time; control over lending policies by banks to lower the cost of capital to smaller firms; control over the aggregate advertising budget of large firms; perhaps more control over what is said in advertisements (this is passed over parenthetically); provision for counteradvertising by an impartial source, presumably publicly subsidized if not undertaken by a governmental body; and compulsory standardization of products so that consumers can be assured that products from different manufacturers are equally good. None of these is in the form of strong recommendations, and the language implies small belief in their adequacy if adopted.

Actions taken to implement these controls have their costs, possibly very high costs, and this is acknowledged:

> The policy implications of this finding depend on the social costs of pursuing various public policies as well as the social costs of permitting monopoly to remain. Indeed, if the differential costs that give rise to entry barriers represent real social costs, it may be socially preferable that entry not take place if the higher costs must be borne either by the entrant or by some supporting agency.[3]

But the authors go on immediately to say:

> Even though policies that lead to increased entry may not be desired because of the social costs incurred as a result, the policy problem of high price-cost margins persists. Although policy judgments become more difficult, these circumstances are not cause for arguing that no policy actions should be taken.[4]

Such actions as "setting price ceilings" by regulators in the manner of public utilities are immediately suggested as appropriate to these "natural oligopolies," which are shielded by pecuniary barriers to

---

[3]Comanor and Wilson, *Advertising and Market Power*, p. 245.
[4]Ibid., p. 246.

entry analogous to the increasing returns associated with public utilities.

A similar but more nebulous justification of such actions is hinted at in a reference to the appropriate response to "tacit" collusion. This may be a reference to proposals, such as Carl Kaysen and Donald F. Turner's, to regulate or, at the very least, give firms reason to act so as to avoid challenge and potential detailed regulation when their industry, or product line, displays a high concentration ratio or even where firms are merely large in some absolute sense.[5] When collusion is tacit, it is not related to actual agreements in restraint of trade, or poor service to customers, but to something else that is associated with market structure, something that has at best an inferential connection with monopoly and/or performance, something vaguely felt but not demonstrated to be harmful to the consumer.

The willingness to consider public-utility type regulation of oligopolistic industries is especially important because Comanor and Wilson's chapter 10 finds economies of scale in many industries such that no room exists for enough firms of efficient size to allow competition by their tests. This finding would classify many industries other than the "small group" of heavy advertisers into natural oligopolies subject to bureaucratic regulation of prices, product line, and advertising.

Even those who are persuaded that advertising is a cause of monopoly can believe that these remedies will turn out to be worse than the conditions they are supposed to alleviate. The conventional assumption that government action will benefit consumers has less empirical support than the contrary notion that it is the "mother of trusts" that harms consumers. A broadly based theory that accounts for regulations that remain unexplained by both these hypotheses is described in a later section of this chapter.

Two theories contest the validity of the consumer protection theory of government regulation. All three are summarized and tested against the available evidence by Jordan. The other two can be thought of as perversions of the consumer protection theory as it works out in practical experience, but for whatever reason they predict net costs to consumers from government regulation of the types favored by the critics of advertising.

The contrasting producer protection hypothesis explains regulation as a tool enterprises use to protect themselves from potential rivals

---

[5]Carl Kaysen and Donald F. Turner, *Antitrust Policy, an Economic and Legal Analysis* (Cambridge, Mass.: Harvard University Press, 1959); Donald F. Turner, "Advertising and Competition," *Federal Bar Journal*, vol. 26 (Spring 1966), p. 96; E. H. Chamberlin, *The Theory of Monopolistic Competition*, 8th ed. (Cambridge, Mass.: Harvard University Press, 1962), Appendix E.

and from each other. Regulation results in de facto cartelization, or "monopolization," of formerly competitive or oligopolistic industries.

Supporters of the consumer protection hypothesis often acknowledge engrossment of benefits by producers rather than consumers, but they do not accept it as an independently competing explanation that may be a superior predictor of the consequences of regulation.

The no-effect hypothesis is less popular although it is advanced by two eminent economists, George J. Stigler and Milton Friedman. Their studies suggest small effects, possibly because tests are confined to natural monopolies where regulation was put in place only after private market control had become well established. Certainly, fifty years of regulation of natural monopolies have shown small effects on average price, the existence of price discrimination, and rates of return. Such differences as were found after regulation suggest lower prices for large enterprises at the expense of households, hardly the outcome predicted by a consumer protection theory. The relevance of these studies to the concern of this book is limited because the present issues relate to allegedly oligopolistic, not monopolistic, industries.

Suggested Regulations: Removal of Barriers to Entry

The appropriate questions to ask about alleged barriers to entry are "Do they exist?" and "Is the consumer better served by some workable alternative?" Neither question is easily answered.

Price Discrimination against Smaller Firms: The Case of TV. Comanor and Wilson place the weight of their finding that small firms are damaged by price discrimination on characteristics of the rate structure for television advertising. The rate structure is said to raise the costs of small firms above those charged their larger rivals. A persuasive case to the contrary has been made by John L. Peterman.[6] The Clorox case is instructive because Procter and Gamble was required to divest Clorox after managing it from 1957 to 1967, permitting comparison of premerger with postmerger sales expense. The interested reader will find substantial support for Peterman's conclusion:

> It is my position that, to the extent the case rests on television rate structures, it is based on a fundamental misconception of their character (and of the markets for time); that these rate structures are not (nor were they) discriminatory according to the buyer's size; and that to the extent discounts are based on

---

[6]John L. Peterman, "The Clorox Case and the Television Rate Structure," *Journal of Law and Economics*, vol. 11 (October 1968), pp. 321–423.

cost differences, they do not seem sufficiently large to cause FTC concern.[7]

The last point merits comment. If price differences exist, but reflect real costs, social costs are less if the differences do affect resource use, including the number of managements (firms) and the constellation of products a given firm in a given area produces. But economies of scale for one input do not necessarily lead to monopoly in output markets or in industries purchasing the input. If they did, all industries using significant amounts of electricity, for example, would be monopolies, perhaps subsidiaries of the power companies. Rather, it is in the interest of producers of such a good to find ways to keep total costs low and net revenues high by pricing in such a way as to reduce use at peak hours, weeks, or months when the good is economically very scarce and to encourage greater use at times of days, weeks, or months during the year when there is less demand. To do so makes the "physically identical" product available at costs that inevitably differ according to time of day and year. But the differing money costs reflect and reduce social cost. Thus lower prices at certain times of day or for services that can be interrupted, or for certain less satisfactory weeks, are not discriminatory but instead are appropriately priced economically and socially different goods that are only superficially the same. Quantity purchases of such goods save costs but also require taking them at times and places that lower average value to the purchaser.

It is not at all obvious that a TV station has a motive to price so as to place small buyers at a disadvantage, especially since there are many stations and several networks to say nothing of rival media with space to fill. Instead, one expects to find innovations such as "participations" that enable small advertisers to obtain commercial time within program series without having to finance a substantial proportion of the total costs involved. Peterman describes this device.[8]

Comanor and Wilson specifically review Peterman's statistical analysis and compute additional regressions using his data. They find that the "principal source of any cost advantage to large-scale television advertisers is quantity discounts on programs,"[9] where a 10 percent increase in the number of messages increases costs only about 7.5 percent. But they go on immediately to note that although larger advertisers could take advantage of these rates by concentrating their programming, they have not done so. Comanor and Wilson speculate that reduced marginal effectiveness of concentrated purchases as

---

[7]Ibid., p. 396.

[8]Ibid., pp. 367–76.

[9]Comanor and Wilson, *Advertising and Market Power*, p. 59.

55

compared with diversification across programs may account for this.

This set of facts suggests that the price differences are not inconsistent with corresponding differences in social costs, and in any case they do not harm smaller firms since they are not used. Instead, stations could save on costs if only they could attract heavier use of given programs by a given advertiser, but the cost savings are too small to offset the lower quality of the marginal messages to the advertiser. If this is correct, there is no discrimination involved in the offer, nor would there be if it were accepted, because it reflects differences in quality. Comanor and Wilson go further, noting that with the exception of NBC, small advertisers do not pay more than large, and conclude, circumspectly, that the evidence is only suggestive that quantity discounts may contribute to economies of scale in advertising and that scale economies may result from price discrimination practiced by some media even if not by all. [10] Unfortunately, these scholarly caveats may be ignored by those with an interest in regulating private enterprises, especially large ones, such as the television networks.

Provision of Impartial Information versus Partial Advertising. Critics of advertising deplore self-interested advertising as deceptive regarding quality. They also believe that it produces virtually valueless differentiations of products that raise costs to consumers with no corresponding increase in quality. It is seen as incompatible with the ideal of well-informed, self-reliant consumers, because they are not able to cope with technically sophisticated products slyly advertised by those who have an interest in selling them. Critics of advertising would assist the consumer by providing impartial information about products and/or by insisting upon the standardization of products.

There are serious difficulties with such suggestions from the consumer viewpoint. One has only to read any copy of *Consumer Reports* to sympathize with the difficulty an impartial authority will encounter in trying to inform consumers intelligently and impartially about product characteristics suitable for differing needs and wants. Since consumers are not standardized by height, weight, age, taste, health, urban-rural, climate, intelligence, mechanical ability, wealth, value of their time, and many other relevant dimensions, it is most difficult to describe cogently the comparative merits of a wide variety of similar products. The problem is compounded when, as is often the case, the desired characteristics depend upon the attitudes and responses of others with whom one comes in contact, others who may or may not reveal their true feelings, as in the case of perfumes, soaps, and wines to take three items from the eight where advertising-to-sales ratios are high. It is no

---

[10]Ibid., p. 61.

less difficult to see how consumer interest is served by standardizing products in such lines, or any other among the eight heavy advertisers. There is also a demand for newness and variety for its own sake that consumers are willing to pay for at times without, necessarily, displacing standard brands that can sell for less because they have smaller risk premiums.

Something of a countercase can be made in favor of partial information as opposed to private or government-supported impartial information. The Sears catalogue may be the best single example of partial, self-interested product information in a literary form widely distributed by a very large private enterprise. *Consumer Reports* is perhaps the best of the self-consciously impartial sources. The former provides partial information but offers a variety of goods serving very similar wants and a money-back guarantee on all of them. Dissatisfied customers are a costly burden on a company, and the merchandise offered in the catalog is a competitive threat to many suppliers and retailers. This has a disciplining effect on prices, quality, and terms of sale that is more detailed, flexible, and unremitting than that any impartial agency can be expected to provide.

Consumer Reports serves a useful purpose, but it is unavoidably irresponsible in the legal sense of the term because it can offer no equivalent to a money-back guarantee. Its creditability as an impartial source is tenuously based on negatives, such as the refusal to carry advertising, and on a nurtured (one might even say "advertised") public skepticism of commercial businesses. These must serve as tokens of impartiality, that is, the impossibility of buying a good rating and a sturdy unwillingness to give a bad rating to a good product because its maker espouses racist, sexist, political, economic, or some other cause the product-raters find abhorrent. Consumers Union's survival without subsidy is the best evidence that these assurances carry weight with many consumers.

Government or government-supported provision of information alleged to be impartial is unavoidably more suspect than a private source such as Consumers Union, which must serve its members to survive. Unfortunately, the past record of government undermines hope that products would be promptly and fairly tested or that the results would be made known in a manner unbiased by political or diplomatic considerations. This is so in part because the power to give or withhold a favorable report has a large cash value that attracts the type of person who will use that power. There is no economic constraint comparable to Consumers Union's life or death need to preserve creditability. The same power can be used to reward or discipline political friends and enemies. It can be used to encourage or discourage foreign competitors in U.S. markets, and so it can be a source of international frictions. Even if honestly and fairly used, government-certified impartial information can have directly perverse effects. John McGee informs this writer that the warning placed on cigarette packages, for example, seems to reduce the liability of tobacco companies. Likewise, air bags in automobiles can be expected to increase "accidents" due to high speed and games of "chicken" if safety claims made for the devices are believed.

Standardization of Products. Mandated elimination of product variety ("differentiation") would greatly ease the government's problem of providing impartial information about products. But its benefits to consumers are dubious indeed.

Virtually nothing recommends the introduction of prior quality control to limit the variety of products and to make each subtype uniform from all producers simply because they are economically distributed with the aid of high advertising-to-sales ratios. The eight discovered by the present analysis—soft drinks, malt liquors, wines, cereals, soaps, clocks and watches, drugs, and perfumes—gain interest and value because of their variety.

The one class of products among these to which prior quality control has been applied, and with the best reason, is drugs.[11] Yet the regulation of drugs is highly controversial and for good reasons. One reason has to do with the protection of the potential consumer's health. It seems entirely reasonable that a drug be certified safe and effective, and that drugs that are not both should be excluded from sale. But neither safety nor effectiveness is knowable in an absolute sense for all people in all conditions. With regard to safety, it is well known that some people have a high tolerance for substances that produce a devastating allergic response in others. With regard to effectiveness, the placebo effect of supposedly ineffective substances is undeniable. The matter of safety and effectiveness is not the only consideration, and often not even the most relevant one. A person with full knowledge of the consequences may prefer to take a risk in order to achieve something of more value to him. Thus a person who simply likes sweets may prefer a low calorie sweetener even if it carries some small risk of, say, cancer. Perhaps his family has a record of heart attacks at the age of forty-five. To reduce weight and avoid heart attacks, he could reduce food intake, and avoid cyclamates, saccharin, and free sugar, none of which is of "proven effectiveness" against overweight. But he *wants* to enjoy sweet flavors. Moreover, he wants more

---

[11]For an excellent survey, see Sam Peltzman, *Regulation of Pharmaceutical Innovation* (Washington, D.C.: American Enterprise Institute, 1974).

sweeteners and fewer calories. The aggressive puritan will say that he should not like sweet flavors, or that he should control his intake for the sake of his health. But this rather arrogant view simply asserts that he should adopt the value system of his critic.

It is one thing to attempt to persuade, but today it is the law that a "drug" can be banned if not proved safe, at least in some dimensions, such as not being carcinogenic. Even if safe, it must be proved effective in some medical sense, such as being valuable in inducing weight loss. Not only can it be banned from production, but the mere possession can be a criminal offense. This is a form of domination that involves a wholesale imposition of the aggressive puritan's values on the rest of the inhabitants of the nation. It is a strong form of *in loco parentis* for all adults.

It is not easy to establish any rule defining the extent to which government should override the preferences of a minority, or a majority, of its citizens, its resident aliens, and others within its jurisdiction. Expert opinion seems to agree that the use of alcohol, tobacco, and sugar is not needed for health and that excessive use is injurious. Yet each is very much desired by many people in virtually every culture, many of whom believe the experts' opinions. People do indulge their taste for such products even when they are forbidden. For that reason it is desirable that less dangerous substitutes be found and made available through normal, noncriminally organized channels where possible. Legislation such as the Delaney amendment frustrates this substitution.

Government Regulation Concentrates Power. The power that agencies such as the Food and Drug Administration wield over the availability of goods desired by consumers is matched by the power it can bring in favor of one industry over another. Power is always enhanced by making apparently illogical or unpopular decisions stick. The decisions on cyclamates make the power of the Food and Drug Administration creditable elsewhere. Cyclamates remain banned in the United States despite continued widespread use abroad, which has produced abundant clinical evidence and laboratory findings that do not replicate the findings that led to the original ban. Yet the ban stands, and is exacerbated by the proposed ban on saccharin.

This power can be used in other directions. A distressing but often heard argument has the bureaucrats serving the interest of the sugar industry by banning two of its major substitutes, cyclamates and saccharin. Although the motivations of these bureaucrats may be of the highest order, the ban on saccharin and cyclamates surely does assist the U.S. and world sugar industry far more than it helps the consumers who like sweets and would also like to avoid sugar. Such power would be absent under competition, where government is free to persuade and warn, but not to criminalize goods and services that are popular substitutes for the products of major industries.

All forms of competition weaken power of large political and economic organizations over consumers. The Delaney amendment, which compels the agency to act on the basis of minimal findings, is ideally suited to the interests of the sugar industry because it goes far beyond putting producers of cyclamates and saccharin in the awkward position of having the healthfulness of their products questioned.

Standardization of products and official control of quality to make the products of rival producers identical can only, on balance, diminish the vitality and interest in everyday living. It is also likely not to aid small firms against the giants who are better able to cope with bureaucratic government. Standardization and prior quality control raise the costs of product development to the detriment of small firms.

The size of the welfare loss that can be attributed to excessive advertising, if any exists at all, cannot exceed 2 percent of the value added in consumer industries; it cannot rationally justify these extreme remedies, if the objective is to benefit consumers.

Regulation of "Natural Oligopoly." According to Comanor and Wilson, regulation to prevent price discrimination against smaller firms by suppliers of essential services, provision of impartial information to consumers, and standardization of products across firms are not enough to ensure "competitive markets" if large firms have a cost advantage. When larger firms have lower costs, "natural oligopoly" is said to exist and government regulation is justified. The test for natural oligopoly is a minimum efficient firm size larger than the average size of the firms ranked fifth to eighth in its industry.[12] This implies that there is room for less than eight efficient-sized firms unless the largest firms, some of which are larger than needed for efficiency by this test, can be broken up. Even then, there is essentially no hope for a large enough number of firms to meet conventional tests for competitive structure.

Industries that may be natural oligopolies comprise a large proportion of the forty-one consumer goods industries in Comanor and Wilson's sample. No less than seventeen and perhaps twenty-nine of them fit this category—somewhere between 41 percent and 71 percent of them. Twelve industries are not natural oligopolies because the statistical procedure failed to determine a minimum efficient size of

---

[12]Comanor and Wilson, *Advertising and Market Power*, p. 225.

firm or plant.[13] Two industries with "excessive" advertising (wines and clocks and watches) and one with marginally excessive advertising (costume jewelry) are among these. All the other industries said to have excessively high advertising-to-sales ratios (except drugs) are in the group where easier entry does not promise competitive structure.

Comanor and Wilson face up to this problem. They declare that these circumstances are not a cause for arguing that no policies should be undertaken. As already noted, the lines of action to be considered center on increased regulation of the public utility type. This has come to include officially monitored entry via certificates of convenience and necessity or franchises and rate making by official bodies. Such bodies also blockade exit when investments sour or opportunities look better elsewhere.

Willingness to consider this type of regulation for soft drinks, malt liquors, cereals, soaps, and perfumes calls into question the bases for judgment used by Comanor and Wilson. It is difficult to think of five consumer goods industries where less damage will be done to the consumer because of ignorance resulting from infrequent purchases or technological sophistication of products that make him gullible. Still, it may be argued, regulation is a sort of low cost insurance policy that at least will do no harm to consumers. The evidence from past regulation, however, is not encouraging.

Estimates of the Effect of Government Regulation on Consumer Welfare

Critics of advertising rarely investigate the effects of current and past regulation of enterprises on consumer welfare. Consequently, their recommendations, or suggestions, imply improvement only to those willing to accept an unexamined alternative. Some industries have been regulated for decades and have produced a record open to examination. Generally, they are industries where protective regulation promised larger gains in efficiency and lower prices, or greater quality improvement, than the industries that Comanor and Wilson now nominate for regulation. Two careful studies of these industries are summarized here. Both provide evidence that consumer interest suffers when regulation is imposed. The loss is much larger than the welfare losses attributable to private monopoly.

William A. Jordan's Analysis of Three Regulated Industries. Jordan summarizes eight studies of three regulated industries—interstate air-

---

[13]Ibid., p. 228.

lines, motor freight carriers, and railroads.[14] Each is competitive or oligopolistic. Some aspects have been deregulated after a period of regulation. Also, because of our federal system, regulated interstate systems have sometimes been in competition with less regulated intrastate systems. Consequently, one can investigate experience under both regulation and market conditions and the effects of deregulation as well as regulation. The evidence that comes from these studies is particularly relevant to a recommendation that public-utility type regulation be extended to additional natural oligopolies in order to benefit the consumer. Jordan's analysis of the eight studies of these industries leads him to this conclusion:

> The available evidence regarding the effects of regulation on the price level for formerly oligopolistic industries is consistent and unambiguous. Regulatory actions and procedures have allowed the carriers in each industry to reach agreements regarding prices and to enforce adherence to these agreements. The result has been substantial increases in price levels for interstate airlines, the freight motor carriers, and the railroads. Without regulation, prices would be from 9 to 50 percent lower than they are with regulation, with many reductions in the long run exceeding 30 percent.[15]

It is noteworthy that price discrimination did not begin in the motor freight industry until *after* it became regulated in 1935, and that although entry is tightly controlled, it has ambiguous effects on profits because costs rise as much as prices. Inefficiencies exist because of controls that increase empty back hauls, prohibit service of intermediate points by some carriers, and for other reasons that increase the quantity of equipment and personnel above that needed to do the job.

Regulation turned out to be a basis from which monopolization could proceed. Whatever potential benefits might have been possible because of possible economies of scale were lost to a kind of rivalrous competition like that attributed to unregulated private oligopolists by critics of oligopolistically and monopolistically competitive free markets. Control of costs is lost in the scramble to obtain favorable regulatory acts. Prices come to be officially determined by costs inflated by the regulatory process itself.

Richard A. Posner's Analysis of the Social Costs of Publicly Regulated and Private Monopoly. Posner has collected various estimates made of price increases attributed to regulation and compared them

---

[14]Jordan, "Producer Protection," pp. 151–76.
[15]Ibid., p. 167.

with increases due to cartel pricing.[16] The studies cited are all from recognized scholars. They agree with Jordan's findings. The price increases under regulation are: physicians' services, 40 percent; eyeglasses, 34 percent; motor carriers, 62 percent; milk, 11 percent; oil (under 1970 import controls), 65 percent; and airlines, 66 percent.[17] Note that the first three are produced by thousands of small producers who would be without monopoly power in the absence of government regulation. Note especially that these can be expected to meet the litmus test for competition, marginal cost equals price, whether or not they are regulated. Since no competitor is large enough to produce a significant portion of the output of the industry, each will expand sales until added cost equals price, so as to maximize net income. The number of milk producers, and the ease of entry into that industry, especially if unregulated, also closely approaches practical definitions of a competitive market. Even oil, despite the size of the companies involved, is one of the least concentrated of American industries; the largest firm produces only 10 percent of U.S. industry output, and there are several in the next largest size, about 5 percent. Evidently there are no economies likely to be attained by central management of these industries. But such claims are used to justify public-utility type regulation.

The price increases attributed by research scholars to private, mostly international, cartels are comparable to those of government-regulated industries in the United States. The estimates are: nitrogen, 75 percent; sugar, 30 percent; aluminum, 100 percent and 38 percent; rubber, 100 percent; electric bulbs, 37 percent; copper, 31 percent; and cast-iron pipe, 39 percent.[18] Antitrust activities may have forestalled losses of these magnitudes by preventing or inhibiting the development of comparable private cartels in the United States. But regulation of a public-utility type is something else. There is little basis in economic theory and, apparently, no basis in experience for expecting benefits to consumers to result from government regulation of prices and entry in any industry other than natural monopolies, if even there.[19]

The strongest case for regulation can be made where economies of scale continue to a point where the whole market is most efficiently served by a single firm—a condition known as "natural monopoly."

---

[16]Posner, "Social Costs of Monopoly and Regulation," pp. 807–27.

[17]Ibid., p. 818.

[18]Ibid., p. 820.

[19]Curiously, government officials sometimes attempt to justify regulation in terms of jobs. The fallacy of composition dominates this justification. Inefficiency has at most an indirect effect on unemployment. It has a direct effect on production and cost of living.

Rivalrous advertising is not among the possible causes of natural monopoly. But even in the case of natural monopolies, the case for regulation is wobbly at best. Large industrial consumers apparently have benefited at the expense of smaller industrial consumers and households under regulation as compared with private discriminating monopoly. Moreover, the monopoly position of a franchised regulated firm is stronger than one whose position rests solely on a cost basis.[20] All the points made thus far contradict the consumer protection theory of regulation.

The basic trouble with the use of government powers to set prices, standardize products and sales techniques, or to simplify and control any other tools of business, is that the potential for monopoly is increased with no assurance whatsoever that the centralized authority will, or can if it tries, serve the varied particular needs and wants of the citizenry. Once a general constitutional limitation of the role of government in business affairs is breached, both public and private economic interests have a new field of opportunity opened to them. The initial flow through the break in the levee is small, but the flood that follows is not. The breach has occurred. Academic critics who have confidence in the consumer protection theory of government regulation may widen it enormously.

An Extended Profit-maximizing Theory of Government Regulation of Business

The producer protection theory implied by the preceding analysis is not satisfactory because it assumes that regulation is sought by business. This sometimes happens, but much modern regulation is resisted. In the sphere of production, all economic life can be described as efforts by individuals and businesses to establish monopolies. In market economics there is free entry into the business of trying to establish a monopoly. But free enterprise guarantees that successful monopolists will be imitated and that monopolies that do not offer comparatively better service per dollar to their customers will not survive in the absence of government assistance. It is natural that government assistance be sought. Government is the only agency that can provide a lasting refuge. Since government-based monopoly is more secure against entry than private monopoly, it will be better able to maintain prices under adverse circumstances. Government can more effectively inhibit entry of new rivals and expansion of service by existing rivals that would drive prices down. A private group of

---

[20]Jordan, "Producer Protection," pp. 160–61.

oligopolists cannot hope to be as effective using only such weak and costly devices as advertising and product differentiation. Therefore, an earnest effort to enlist government support by firms facing efficient competitors must be expected. Any persuasive argument that assists this activity will be used. This is the basis for the producer protection theory.

But why should government assist firms or industries seeking protection? Thinking up successful arguments is one area of innovation by business. Two arguments that have won government assistance in the past include cutthroat competition, including imports from foreign producers (with attendant instability), and inappropriateness of commercial motivation. Both are justified by the rhetoric of consumer protection. Thus railroads are regulated ostensibly to provide equitable and stable rates and good service not provided by competition among firms with high total but low marginal costs; and many professions, including doctors, lawyers, pharmacists, and optometrists are regulated so as to provide high quality services to consumers presumably technically unable to judge for themselves their needs and alternatives. All such regulation can be viewed to some degree as disappointing and, to an extent, as examples of perversions of the consumer protection theory.

Neither the producer protection theory nor the consumer protection theory explains the current proliferation of controls over environmental pollution, occupational safety, equal opportunity, and affirmative action. Nor are these programs so beneficial to the majority of consumers, viewing their interests from a private point of view, as to induce anything more than passive support. Majority opposition is more probable. The success of these types of regulation becomes explicable if one considers the possibility that the initial impetus favoring regulation need not, and very often does not, come from business, labor, or consumer interests, but rather from some other interest group that prepares the way so as eventually to enlist the efforts of those needed to put it across. The notion that a normal function of government is to adjust the institutional structure so as to constrain managers to approximate fulfillment of the economic criteria for efficiency is part of our common intellectual property. The key additional element needed is an *idea* that associates some "remedy" with an improvement that enhances what is thought of as the general welfare. Welfare economics would seem to be an obviously appropriate source of persuasive ideas.

The work of economic theorists may be accomplished for the usual rewards of scholarship. Their theorems become the common property of economists working in applied fields and part of the intellectual equipment of professional, business, and governmental managers. Thus the innovator of an idea upon which a new government policy that meets these criteria can be based has a potentially receptive audience not only among government officials and bureaucrats but also among some of those to be regulated. The innovator, therefore, has a potential vehicle for accomplishing praiseworthy objectives and reaping suitable rewards. These considerations provide a base for regulations that are incompatible with the producer protection hypothesis viewed as regulations instigated by business.

Probably the most far-reaching innovation in recent times based on and in part promoted by economists is the politically potent discovery of pervasive "externalities" that might be put right by taxation, subsidies, establishing new property rights, or by regulation. The outstanding fact is that regulation frequently has been chosen from the range of choices although few businesses can hope to benefit in the first instance because the regulations are not organized around industries that may directly gain monopoly power from the regulation, but rather are organized around particular departments or aspects of many industries. This type of regulation is distinguished from other types by a forthright acceptance of higher costs and prices by those advocating and those administering the regulation. President Carter's energy policy is only an extreme example of this kind of regulation. The increased cost is defended as less than the increased social benefits, which, however, are often declared to be too precious to be assigned values that can be compared to costs at all. This is troublesome because it asserts a fanatic position that leaves no room for alternative values or opinions. Nevertheless, this assault on the legitimacy of private wants sometimes succeeds.

Business and trade union opposition to this type of regulation is often short-lived, having the character of a rearguard or holding operation after which acceptance and cooperation is forthcoming. Business and labor are at first reluctant to accept regulations formulated by Congress or regulatory bodies in response to nonunion or antiunion, often antibusiness, groups. Changes originating from unpredictable academic or hostile political groups threaten their security. Nevertheless, once regulation seems virtually certain, every firm and labor organization likely to be regulated needs to cooperate so that it can exercise some control over the new arrangements. There are also potential gains. The regulations make the regulators, to a degree, responsible for the economic health of their charges. They become a demi-resource, whose actions are as important for the firm's success as the availability of capital. Regulators are prone to appeals to avoid redundant capacity by limiting entry. Other regulations can be expected to reduce risks for existing firms. The fact is that government regulation makes feasible and acceptable actions that would be illegal and subject to intense disapprobation if accomplished by private agreement and contracting. It legitimizes them, certifying the union of social values with private activities.

The cost of establishing new enterprises, hiring a proper racial balance of employees, and penetrating existing markets with new products is substantially raised by regulation of the type implicitly or explicitly supported by the critics of advertising. They raise a substantial barrier to new entry, protecting existing firms, allowing them to secure prices sufficient to cover their increased costs and perhaps more. Thus government regulation may become the foundation for the protection of established producers. The protection has small, more likely negative, value to consumers. As already observed, higher costs due to gaining compliance, inefficiency, delayed improvements, and higher profits have negative effects. It is hard to see any net benefits for consumers from higher costs.

A Case for Advertising by Oligopolists

The arguments that government intervention to establish competitive conditions can benefit consumers rest on a view of the world that mistakes a simplified formal model of economic reality for a feasible reality and that ignores the sociological equivalent for the Heisenberg principle, that the intervention itself changes the process. This is investigated more carefully in Chapter 4. At this point only an initial sampling of substantial competition among U.S. industries and the procompetitive effects of advertising are presented. Then follows a positive suggestion for government action that can improve quality of competition and benefit consumers further.

Evidence of Competition from Studies of Demand Elasticity. Basically, demand elasticity is calculated by dividing the percentage change of quantity sold by the percentage change of price associated with the change in quantity. The change in price needs to be relatively small if ambiguity is to be avoided and "other things," such as the money incomes of actual and potential customers and the availability and cost of substitutes and complementary goods, should not change. Since more is sold at lower prices, the ratio has a negative sign and produces a coefficient that varies between 0.0, where the quantity does not change at all when the price is higher or lower, to minus infinity, where an indefinitely large quantity is taken at a slightly lowered price and none if price is raised slightly. In a sense, the midpoint is -1.0, where

67

the percent change in quantity is the same as the percent change in price. This is called "unit elasticity," and it leaves total revenue unchanged when price changes. Common terminology calls elasticities between −1.0 and minus infinity "elastic" and refers to them as being "higher" in the sense of "more elastic." Elasticities between −1.0 and 0.0 are termed "inelastic." An inelastic demand curve yields a higher *total* revenue at higher prices.

The common-sense belief (or superstition) seems to be that all demand curves are highly inelastic. This is rarely true of the demand for an individual firm's production, because many buyers soon shift to other producers in the industry. But most *industrywide* demand curves are inelastic. Therefore, if firms successfully collude to form an effective monopoly, they often raise their total revenues by producing less. Producing less not only saves costs, but actually increases *total* revenues when demand is inelastic. Output reduction will continue until an elastic segment of the demand curve is penetrated. *Thus, production at an inelastic point on the industry demand curve is indirect evidence that the industry is not effectively monopolized.*

Most industry demand curves calculated by econometricians have low elasticities. Comanor and Wilson find the demand elasticities for twenty-two of the thirty-six industries—61 percent for which they could compute long-run elasticities—to be inelastic (0.0 to −1.0) and nine (25 percent) to have elasticities between −1.0 and −2.0. This is roughly in line with other studies. This author collected all the estimates he could find and reported them elsewhere.[21] Sixty-three products (66 percent) had elasticities between 0.0 and −0.999; twenty-five (26 percent), between −1.0 and −2.0, and eight had elasticities greater than −2.0. There are good reasons why firms have trouble forming an effective collusive agreement when they lack the aid of government. Three difficult problems must be solved. It is necessary to find a way to share the profit among existing producers, to find ways to keep each from selling too much, and to keep potential producers from entering the market.

Higher elasticities are at least consistent with "shared monopoly," but they cannot reasonably be counted as indirect evidence favoring this hypothesis. Profits for every firm in the industry can be increased if the demand curve for the industry is less elastic than the demand curves facing the individual firms. Positive evidence of monopoly requires either a close correspondence between the elasticities facing individual firms and the industry elasticity, or price-cost markups that are consistent with the industrywide elasticity of demand. If the indus-

---

[21]Worcester, "On Monopoly Welfare Losses," table 1, p. 1016.

try elasticity is −1.0, the implied marginal cost is zero and markup over cost is

$$\frac{\text{Price} - \text{Marginal Cost}}{\text{Marginal Cost}} = \text{Infinity}.$$

If industry elasticity is −2.0, the markup should be 100 percent over costs and so on. This is analyzed further in Chapter 4.

The complete list with elasticities high enough to support even the possibility of effective monopoly, taken as −1.5 or lower, are given in Table 8, along with the profit rates for the industries reported by Comanor and Wilson. An elasticity of −1.5 is surely extreme because it implies prices three times marginal costs and, most likely, enormous profits on equity. A priori expectations suggest the absence of monopolistic prices in most cases where industrywide demand elasticity is greater than −1.5. But some may be suspect. Four of the eight industries have advertising-to-sales ratios over 5 percent and demands more elastic than −1.5. Of these, cereals, drugs, and soft drinks have profits higher than the unweighted average of 7.9 percent for the forty-one industries. Their profits are still small as compared with the potential implied by their industry demand elasticities. Perhaps more significant is the absence of such popular whipping boys as oil production and refining, steel, automobile, and aluminum production from the list of industries with high elasticities.

It is clear, however, and significant that demand conditions exist that facilitate efforts to monopolize most industries. The elasticity of industry demand for many goods and services is between −1.0 and 0.0. Restriction of industry output would increase total revenues and inevitably increase the total incomes of those producing the product. Government regulation that "rationalizes" the industry for any reason can help capture these profits. Several branches of government have reason to oblige. Some of the profits from higher prices paid by consumers can be siphoned off in licenses and fees to pay for the regulators or for taxes to fatten the government treasury while still leaving additional profits in the hands of the existing firms. Unions may obtain much of the gain for the employees who are needed to produce the reduced output. The burden is borne by would-be rival producers, whose activities would lower prices and provide more choices to consumers were they allowed by the regulators to compete, by the workers excluded from employment in the monopolized industries, and, of course, by the consumers.

Although few firms presently have, or seem to have, a desire to establish government regulation of their prices, government control of entry undoubtedly can be far more effective than anything obtainable

Table 8

Industries Having
Elasticities of Demand Less Than −1.5

Industry	Elasticity	Profit[a] (percent)
Clocks and watches[b]	−9.802	1.9
Tomatoes (fresh)	−4.6	
Millinery	−4.165	−1.3
Foreign travel, U.S. residents	−4.1	
Medical care and hospital insurance	−3.6	
Costume jewelry	−3.275	1.4
Interest on personal debt	−2.7	
Intercity railway	−2.7	
Green peas (fresh)	−2.8	
Cigars	−2.457	5.3
Cigarettes[c]	−2.457	11.5
Tomatoes (canned)	−2.5	
Airline travel	−2.4	
Grain mill products	−2.099	7.0
Cereals[b,c]	−2.099	14.8
Lamb, retail	−1.8 to −2.0	
Instruments	−1.958	12.0
Nondurable toys	−1.7	
Drugs[b]	−1.695	14.0
Automobile insurance	−1.6	
Green peas (canned)	−1.6	
Electrical appliances	−1.567	10.3
Soft drinks[b]	−1.540	10.0
Peaches, retail	−1.5	
Watermelons	−1.5	
Shoe cleaning and repairs	−1.5	
Auto, retail	−0.8 to −1.5	

[a] The simple average profit rate for the forty-one industries is 7.91 percent.
[b] Among the eight industries with high advertising-to-sales ratios.
[c] This industry was consolidated with the industry listed directly above in figuring elasticity, for example, cigars and cigarettes.

Sources: All with profit rates, Comanor and Wilson, *Advertising and Market Power*, pp. 89–90, 134–35. Others from Worcester, "On Monopoly Welfare Losses," p. 1016.

by advertising or with currently feasible agreements. Consequently, business opposition to government regulation based upon such "objective" measures as some combination of advertising-to-sales ratio, minimum economic size of firm (or plant), and concentration ratio, may well turn out to be short-lived and halfhearted. It matters little to consumers whether the profits endure or are consumed in reduced efficiency, higher costs due to satisfying regulatory agencies, taxes, or enlarged factor costs. The higher prices will endure or rise further in any of these events.

The prospects for improved profits due to regulation are not particularly good for the eight industries with high advertising-to-sales ratios because the elasticities of their industry demand curves are more frequently elastic than the others. But possibilities exist for them because the elasticity of each individual firm's demand curve is undoubtedly much greater. Regulation also offers smaller gains to these industries than those already regulated because their situation is more complex. Nevertheless, if regulation becomes a likely prospect it is reasonable to predict significant cooperation by these industries even prior to enactment, however damaging it may turn out to be to consumer interests.

Direct Evidence of Advertising as an Antimonopoly Influence. Fortunately, some evidence exists that tests the expectation that advertising is primarily a tool of competition, not monopoly. Careful research of three industries—eyeglasses, prescription drugs, and toys—shows advertising to have a price-lowering effect when quality differences are taken into account. Government actions that prohibit or severely limit advertising resulted in higher prices to consumers of eyeglasses and prescription drugs. Although the results of studies of these industries are highly relevant to an analysis of advertising as it affects industry structure, they are little cited by the critics of advertising and of statistically determined monopolistic or oligopolistic markets.

Lee and Alexandra Benham's analysis of the price of eyeglasses and advertising. The Benhams' study[22] of the American Optometric Association is of special interest here because control of advertising is a primary element in a system of professional control that has sometimes secured state government support. Where achieved, it has increased the price of eyeglasses to consumers no less than 25 percent.

> Professional codes of ethics usually prohibit advertising, limit brand name identification, strongly discourage public evaluation of other professionals' work, and place limitations wherever possible on other public indications of the characteristics, quality, or price of services provided.[23]

---

[22]Lee and Alexandra Benham, "Regulating through the Professions: A Perspective on Information Control," *Journal of Law and Economics*, vol. 18 (October 1975), pp. 421–47.
[23]Ibid., p. 421.

An Oregon court case they cite upheld action against a dentist who advertised in violation of his state's ethical code, the court holding it to be no defense that the advertising statements asserting the dentist's superiority were truthful.

The Benhams reproduce a score sheet used by the Michigan Optometric Association for membership. A score of 85 must be attained in five years or less after scoring no less than 65 initially. Thirty of the possible points are for avoidance of advertising (including media displays), 25 more are for location in a professional or office building that does not carry commercial or discount connotations, and 15 additional points are awarded for limiting office identification signs to approved size and content. That leaves 14 points for engaging in professional education activities, 8 for having suitable facilities, and 8 more for having suitable equipment.

The Benhams argue that these limitations facilitate association control over the activities of its members because the professional judgment of colleagues is made relatively important, even crucial in those cases where loss of membership bars the individual from practice.

But do consumers benefit from the "ethical" control of their memberships by the professional associations? Consumers benefit, it is argued, because professionals are not commercially motivated but instead desire to provide services to those who feel a need for them but who are not competent enough to assess their true needs or to choose intelligently among alternative suppliers. Consumers are said to get better quality service and no unneeded service.

It is possible to make some progress toward an evaluation of this argument because the degree of control of optometrists differs from state to state. The Benhams' statistical analysis finds prices 25 percent to 40 percent higher where professional control and restrictions on advertising are the most stringent. They find little effect of professional control where the consumer is most subject to fraud, the selling of unneeded glasses. The price paid by the less educated, and for that reason those considered more vulnerable to bad advice, is somewhat *higher* than the prices paid by the well educated. The principal effect of the higher prices seems not to be better service, but rather failure of more people needing glasses to get them in the areas where professional control is strongest, probably because of higher cost. The most cautious conclusion that can be drawn from these data is that they do not support a case against advertising and commercial provision of eyeglasses. The implication for other professions is obvious.

John F. Cady's investigation of retail drugs. Cady tests three alternative hypotheses that predict different consequences for drug prices and

72

quality of service by retail druggists with and without advertising.[24] As in the case of eyeglasses, differences in regulations among the states permit comparisons. Those states with strong pharmaceutical associations that have succeeded in prohibiting advertising may have different prices and qualities of service than those where advertising is permitted. A legalized cartel hypothesis predicts higher prices and approximately the same level of service in the states with strong associations; a professional control hypothesis predicts higher prices and better service; and a cost shift hypothesis predicts the same or lower prices for consumers and better service in states with strong associations. A national sample of more than 1900 pharmacies produced data on five dimensions of service quality and prices charged for ten drugs that constitute a representative sample of all drugs dispensed.

Prescription prices averaged 5.2 percent lower in states permitting advertising. Services offered varied greatly by size of pharmacy, but very little between states with two exceptions: the keeping of family records, which were more frequently kept in regulated states; and the provision of emergency services, which were more commonly available in unregulated states. There was no significant difference in the size distribution of pharmacies in the two groups of states.

Cady concludes: "This is the outcome predicted from the *legalized cartel case.* Consumers should therefore benefit substantially from the removal of these price advertising regulations."[25]

Robert L. Steiner's investigation of the advertising of toys. One of the hypotheses that Steiner tests is that:

> Advertising cuts distribution costs on advertised brands for two reasons: (1) advertising causes goods to turn over rapidly so they can be sold profitably with smaller markups; and, (2) advertising creates product identity—which, in differentiated products, permits the public to compare prices between stores, thus setting a limit on the retailer's freedom to mark up. Products which are both heavily advertised and are fast sellers will be pulled through the distribution channels with the lowest markups of all.[26]

Steiner tells us that until the late 1950s U.S. toy-makers advertised very little, but that this changed in the mid-1950s when Mattel bought time on *The Mickey Mouse Club* TV show. Advertising expense rose from

---

[24]John F. Cady, *Restricted Advertising and Competition: The Case of Retail Drugs* (Washington, D.C.: American Enterprise Institute, March 1976).

[25]Ibid., p. 20.

[26]Robert L. Steiner, "Does Advertising Lower Consumer Prices?" *Journal of Marketing,* vol. 37 (October 1973), reprinted by the American Enterprise Institute (Reprint No. 37, January 1976), p. 8 of the reprint.

very low levels to about 3.5 percent of the value of shipments. Analysis of the U.S. and Canadian toy industries shows a substantial reduction in manufacturer's margins from about 49 percent to about 33 percent, probable net cost savings due to larger volume of advertised toys (perhaps 5 percent after allowance for increased advertising costs); a reduction of margins on unadvertised products in the same categories as the heavily advertised ones; and a reduction of toy-makers in the United States to about 700, with the largest selling about 9 percent of the market, and the largest four about 30 percent. (The largest firm has lost money in some years.)

An interesting sidelight is provided by the sale of toy guns after the Vietnam War reduced demand and political passions made advertising them inadvisable in any case. The consequences are summarized by Steiner:

> Innovation at the manufacturer's level has almost stopped. Retailers report both that their cost for toy guns has advanced and that their own mark-ups have fattened. Without television and newspaper advertising, there are virtually no demanded or identifiable items, so the retailer has little to gain from sharp prices and little to fear from inflated ones.[27]

From these studies it seems to make sense for enterprises seeking power to raise prices to work toward some means of discipline that restrains or prohibits advertising. Advertising lowers the prices of toys, eyeglasses, and prescription drugs by enhancing competitive pressures on margins, spurring innovation, and doing so with more reason to improve quality than otherwise. These findings are in basic agreement with the studies of long-term public regulation of other dimensions of business as summarized by Jordan and Posner. On this record, it seems likely that either public regulation or private cartelization of enterprise must be expected to raise prices to consumers with no offsetting increase in quality of product or service. Producers gain from higher prices and savings of advertising expense. They can afford to spend this much to organize and secure government support for their exclusionary activities.

There is no reason to expect regulation to turn out differently if it is imposed by government regulation on some of the eight industries

---

[27]Ibid., p. 17. This substitution relationship between advertising and higher retail margins to compensate retailers for the extra time it takes to satisfy customer queries pervades merchandising. Firms that do not advertise get a cheap ride on rivals' advertising by making it profitable for the retailer to sell his higher margin good to those attracted by highly advertised substitutes. This fact complicates the analysis because it distorts the apparent price-cost margins between advertised and nonadvertised brands. The overall product quality is also different because buyers of unadvertised brands have weaker recourse if the product is not satisfactory.

found by Comanor and Wilson to have excessive advertising-to-sales ratios, or if it is imposed on the seven found by them to have economies of scale in advertising, or if it is imposed on any of the remaining group of industries with firms that produce at less than the most economical scale. *The power to regulate is the power to monopolize. The record of governments is overwhelmingly in favor of "creating jobs" and serving the interests of enterprises that are a part of, or which cooperate with, government. Little regard is paid to inflated costs or to the higher prices charged the ordinary consumer.*

Studies of this type underestimate the value of advertising to consumers because the time consumers spend looking for goods and services is valued at zero. When firms cannot advertise, consumers must bear a larger part of the marketing burden. Restriction of advertising also narrows horizons—knowledge of what is possible or the range of effective desires. Such costs are not counted among social costs because there is no adequate way to measure the value of time spent within the household sector. Therefore, total costs of informing consumers may be lowered even if prices are raised somewhat by advertising. The real costs the consumers bear may be reduced by more than the prices are increased, if they are in fact increased.

A Role for Government in Support of Competition and Consumer Interests

There are things that government can do that will benefit consumers at all income levels. Government can improve the conditions of entry, giving new firms a better chance and thereby keeping old firms keenly alert to developments in their markets rather than to developments in committee rooms of Congress and regulatory agencies. Since, apparently, some people have more confidence in government testing than they do in private testing services, a government agency, such as the Bureau of Standards, could be empowered to test products voluntarily submitted to it and to certify those that performed according to the claims made about them. This certification would add valuable information to the firm's advertising and would put pressures on other firms to do likewise. Endorsement of this kind is particularly valuable to new entrants because this device adds credibility to what might otherwise appear to buyers as inflated self-serving claims made by firms of unknown and therefore unreliable reputation.

Major companies can also benefit, of course. The success of Crest toothpaste following the cautious validation of its effectiveness against tooth decay by the American Dental Association illustrates the potency of this type of impartially supported information. Such endorsement needs to be supplemented with some continuing proof that the products marketed are the same as those tested (within feasible quality control limits), and, of course, care must always be taken to make sure that favorable endorsements are neither bought nor refused for reasons other than product merit. Both of these dangers are minimized when submission of products for testing is voluntary, only affirmative findings can be reported, the products are trademarked and advertised by the producers, private testing agencies continue to exist, and rivals have cause to monitor each other's products and procedures. Suits against agency budgets and personnel for delayed or biased finding should also be effective against corrupt, delayed, or inaccurate testing and validating.

4
Why Welfare Economics
Misleads Policy

This chapter and the next search for the reasons that lead this study to interpretations of statistical findings so much at variance with those held by critics of advertising, monopolistic competition, and oligopoly. These chapters also explain why this study does not accept the remedies that these critics suggest or imply.[1] In part, the difference is found in an inherently defective use of the modern theory of markets. That theory, most valuable as a tool of discovery, is not useful for policy choices. This chapter contends that at present there is no normative economic theory appropriate for making policy decisions. The next chapter attempts to construct the foundation for such a theory.

Theorists have developed a highly refined, abstract theory of economic efficiency, paradoxically named "welfare economics." It is similar to theories in the physical sciences in that it postulates conditions that are only approximated under the intellectual equivalent of laboratory conditions. Thus perfect competition is a concept that is as useful and as unlikely to be encountered in the marketplace as is a perfect vacuum in a workshop. Although essential to the advance of knowledge, such postulates are of indirect, often subtle value for policy decisions and can be misleading. Thus, to continue the analogy, information discovered with the help of hypotheses involving pure vacuums does not imply that the information gained is useful only where pure vacuums exist, or that conditions as close as possible to vacuums should be made to exist, or that physical events should take place as if they existed in a pure vacuum, or that every effort should be made to make events occur as if they were in a pure vacuum by

---

[1] A book that has just come to my attention takes a course closely parallel to the one taken here: Charles K. Rowley and Alan T. Peacock, *Welfare Economics: A Liberal Restatement* (New York: Wiley, 1975).

introducing a number of adjustments so what occurs naturally in a vacuum will be simulated in normal terrestrial circumstances.

Yet criteria taken directly from welfare economics are used by some students of industry structure as criteria for desirable performance that should be simulated if necessary. Competition is made the test of efficiency and is then defined in terms of the mathematical criteria for an optimum price equal to marginal cost and marginal productivities in every dimension equal to every relevant factor cost. A system of private property, free enterprise, and free contracting that is thought by these students not fully to meet such criteria in each industry is deemed "less competitive" than a centrally planned economy that does. Even then, an intellectual leap is required to take such real or imagined failures as evidence, even on paper, that citizens' desires, the ostensible objective of competition, are more meticulously served by simulated formal competitive arrangements.

A Neglected Fundamental Question

Formal economic theory makes use of strong hypotheses in order to gain clarity and efficiency. A competitive market is defined as having homogeneous divisible products and large numbers of buyers and sellers possessed of perfect knowledge. These clean concepts, necessary for orderly mathematical manipulation, produce testable hypotheses of enormous value for advancing knowledge, the primary function of "positive" economics. But they are serious hindrances to useful policy making. Departure from one or more of these idealized conditions is often seen as requiring monopoly theorizing and as justifying direct government intervention to establish or simulate competition. But as Stigler says,

> These extreme assumptions are not *necessary* to the existence of competition: it is sufficient, for example, if each trader knows a fair number of buyers and sellers, if all traders together have comprehensive knowledge so only one price rules. The reason for not stating the weakest assumptions (necessary conditions) for competition is that they are difficult to formulate, and in fact are not known precisely.[2]

This section begins the search for weak assumptions appropriate for

---

[2]George S. Stigler, *Theory of Price* (New York: Macmillan, 1966), p. 89. Stigler has since modified the one price rule in consideration of the different position of different households and firms. See Stigler and Gary S. Becker, "De Gustibus Non Est Disputandum," *American Economic Review*, vol. 67 (March 1977), pp. 76–91. This article unites firms and households and is compatible with the "normative" analytical model presented in Chapter 5.

policy making where no possible choice meets the formal conditions for an optimum.

The legacy of the 1930s weighs heavily upon economists, making it difficult to avoid the temptation to confer some degree of monopoly power on every producer and with it a need for corrective regulation. But the nature of monopoly power remains clouded with ambiguities. Differences among close substitutes, such as standard models of Fords and Chevrolets, carry the same theoretical significance for utility as differences between goods that serve divergent needs, such as wheat and shoes, if the elasticities of demand (or the coefficients of substitution) are the same. Stigler states the point succinctly: "If a product is not homogeneous, it is meaningless to speak of large numbers. Hence, if every unit is essentially unique (as in the market for domestic servants) there cannot be large numbers." But, he goes on immediately to say: "Yet, if the various units are highly substitutable for one another, the market can approach competition."[3]

Ambiguity is enhanced because it takes time to adjust to change, and, during any short period, prices and qualities of similar products are set by the firms that offer them. This also invalidates a formal requirement for competition: that each individual firm be powerless to affect the price of the good sold, or the inputs purchased, a condition implied even by the weak conditions quoted from Stigler. Under the formal requirements, a firm makes the most if the added cost of producing a little more (the marginal cost) is exactly equal to the price for which it sells. But the presence or absence of this equality is difficult if not impossible to observe. So students of market structure substitute other conditions deduced from the formal theory of monopoly, such as high profits, scarcity of firms in a market, and barriers to entry. This substitution leads away from the evaluation of feasible alternatives to a proliferation of suspected market failures based upon real and imagined discrepancies from the formal idealized model that cannot be attained under any circumstances. Concentration on formal market failures obscures perception of the performances of the actual system that may approximate or even better that expected of the formal model. This chapter tries to evaluate the quality of competition existing in industries that do not meet the formal criteria for competition.

Cost-Price Relationships. As already noted, the textbook test for monopoly is summarized as price in excess of marginal cost. Fully interpreted, it summarizes the set of conditions referred to as Pareto optimality. James M. Ferguson's excellent critical review of the litera-

---

[3]Ibid., p. 88.

ture on advertising and market power accepts this definition. He begins with the statements:

> Monopoly power is the ability to sell at prices above marginal cost. All firms which face downward-sloping demand curves possess monopoly power, because, with a downward-sloping demand, they can set price above marginal cost. . . . However, a downward-sloping demand does not guarantee monopoly profits will be earned. Barriers to entry are necessary.[4]

The relationship between marginal cost and price, and the existence or absence of profits, are confusing and unreliable standards for judging the performance of an economy and for evaluating alternative policies, the essence of analysis for policy making. The plain fact is that none of the alternatives among which a choice can be made meet the highly abstract tests of formal welfare economics. Perhaps the most unfortunate aspect of this formalistic approach is the diversion of investigation away from the examination of property right formation and contracting by private parties, a diversion that allows social and political activists who do not understand the economy to persuade many that critical problems are neglected in market economies when, in fact, they are being handled very well. Recent works by Ronald H. Coase and Steven N. S. Cheung, to name only two, show how far from accurate are those who simply have assumed that "externalities" requiring regulation exist whenever they have encountered (or imagined) a situation where private decisions seem to be wasteful or short-sighted.[5]

Some first class economists have been aware of the inappropriateness of the formal investigative structure for normative judgments and policy analysis virtually from the beginning. Decades ago Alfred Marshall voiced this warning:

> The theory of stable equilibrium of normal demand and supply helps indeed to give definiteness to our ideas; and in its elementary stages does not diverge from the actual facts of life, so far as to prevent its giving a fairly trustworthy picture of the chief methods of action of the strongest and most persistent group of economic forces. But when pushed to its

---

[4]Ferguson, *Advertising and Competition: Theory, Measurement, Fact*, pp. 15–16.

[5]Ronald H. Coase, "The Problem of Social Cost," vol. 3 (October 1960), pp. 1–44; Steven N. S. Cheung, "The Structure of a Contract and the Theory of a Nonexclusive Resource," vol. 13 (April 1970), pp. 49–70; "The Fable of the Bees: An Economic Investigation," vol. 16 (April 1973), pp. 11–34; and "A Theory of Price Control," vol. 17 (April 1974), pp. 53–72, all in *Journal of Law and Economics*.

more remote and intricate logical consequences it slips away from the conditions of real life.[6]

Joseph A. Schumpeter stated it more strongly in 1948:

> The classical theory of monopolistic pricing (the Cournot-Marshall theory) is not entirely valueless, especially when overhauled so as to deal not only with the instantaneous maximization of monopoly gain but also with maximization over time. But it works with assumptions that are so restrictive as to exclude its *direct* application to reality. In particular it cannot be used for what it *is* being used in current teaching, namely, for a comparison between the way in which a purely competitive economy functions and the way in which an economy functions that contains substantial elements of monopoly.[7]

Frederick A. Hayek writes:

> I am far from denying that in our system equilibrium analysis has a useful function to perform. But when it comes to the point where it misleads some of our leading thinkers into believing that the situation which it describes has direct relevance to the solution of practical problems, it is time to remember *that it does not deal with social processes at all* and that it is no more than a useful preliminary to the study of the main problem.[8]

The problem remains very much with us today. The formal conditions for an optimum have become substantially more refined in the thirty years since Schumpeter wrote the quoted passage, but analysts continue to apply them all when considering policy recommendations, acting as if the formal conditions exist or could be made to exist.

One must scrutinize and improve upon the criteria used to judge efficiency in a work devoted to the analysis of the normative characteristics of advertising. The rest of this chapter tries to demonstrate why the formal tests used by Ferguson, Comanor and Wilson, and many others are not useful for this purpose. The next chapter develops a (partial) framework for a more adequate analysis.

---

[6] Alfred Marshall, *Principles of Economics*, 8th ed. (New York: Macmillan, 1920), p. 461.

[7] Schumpeter, *Capitalism, Socialism and Democracy*, 3rd ed., p. x. For a modern treatment of the tendency of concentration and efficiency to be positively related, see McGee, *In Defense of Industrial Concentration*, especially chaps. 5–7. See also D. K. Round, "Industry Structure, Market Rivalry and Public Policy: Some Australian Evidence," *Journal of Law and Economics*, vol. 18 (April 1975), pp. 273–81.

[8] Frederick A. Hayek, "The Price System as a Mechanism for Using Knowledge," in M. A. Bornstein, *Comparative Economic Systems: Models and Cases*, 3rd ed. (Homewood, Ill.: Irwin, 1974), p. 33. Italics added.

The Marginal Cost–Equal Price Test Is Often Irrelevant. If efficiency is desired, the combination of resources that produces a given output with the lowest total cost in resources is preferable to all others. There is no reason in principle, even in formal theory, why a single firm monopolist with a downward-sloping demand curve cannot have the lowest possible total factor costs. If all alternatives have higher costs, it is not just idle to say that the monopolist worsens the efficiency of the economy; it is mischievous.

Nor does the contrary hold. Were every firm unable to affect price and were prices everywhere equal to marginal cost, there would be no guarantee of efficiency. For example, the numerous firms might belong to one or another trade association, each of which successfully limits its numbers. With fewer producers, prices are higher than socially desirable because the firms earn higher than normal returns that do not stimulate more production. Each member of each trade association may, nevertheless (and will, if it maximizes its profits), carry production to the point where marginal cost is equal to price. This is not efficient. Were it possible to dissolve the associations, some presently excluded individuals would transfer from their lower productive, lower paid occupations and efficiency would be improved. Such an association of small firms has harmful market power that impairs efficiency. A single firm monopolist who produces at least social cost does not. The equality of marginal cost to price fails as a guide to efficiency in both cases.

Profits and Price Discrimination as Indicators of Monopoly. These difficulties and others that plague the estimation of marginal costs and the relevant prices have led to the substitution of other tests for misallocation derived from the theory of monopoly. Profit rates and price discrimination are two such. Both are more amenable to being measured and so are often substituted for the relationship between marginal cost and price when attempting to estimate the extent and costs of monopoly power. In principle, the rate of profit will be the same in every industry at equilibrium if competitive markets exist. This is true because people will shift their investments from low profit to higher profit firms until the profit differences vanish.

Profits do differ from industry to industry and from firm to firm, and it is entirely reasonable to suppose that high profit rates will be obtained by exercise of monopoly power. But monopoly is not the only source of higher than average reported profits. They can exist and persist because of higher than average special risks, such as sensitivity of sales to cyclical fluctuations, rapid product obsolescence, or vulnerability to weather, to name a few of the many real costs that cannot be shown as costs and so are covered out of "profits."

One way to get at this difficulty is to allow for a range of normal profits and to consider only those that exceed the upper bound as more probably caused by monopoly. This author attempted this using the data for firms as reported in the *Fortune* 500 for the years 1956 through 1969.[9] During those years, 562 firms appeared among the 500 five or more times. The competitive rate of profit for each year was assumed to be 90 percent of the median profit rate on invested capital for the 500. A calculated competitive rate 5 percent or more below the actual rate was taken as presumptive evidence that the firm in question enjoyed monopoly profits. Since temporary disturbances cause short-run fluctuations in profits that are quickly corrected, it was assumed that monopoly profits of interest to social critics and policy makers would exist only if this test for monopoly were met over a period of time. On this basis, a firm was counted as "monopolistic" if it appeared in the *Fortune* list ten or more of the fourteen years included in the study and met the above test for monopoly profits six or more years, or appeared at least six times and met the test for monopoly returns every year it appeared. Thirty companies made this list.[10] They include nine drug, two glass, two photographic, and two food companies. In most cases, other companies producing similar products were among the largest 500.

The composition of this list raises doubt about the appropriateness of my test for monopoly. Some companies, such as IBM, Xerox, and Polaroid may have had monopoly profits, but their profits are based on a combination of remarkable innovation and patent protection designed to encourage exactly their kinds of risky expansion based on the putting of new ideas to uses that enhance efficiency and spread benefits widely throughout society. Much the same thing can be said of the drug companies. By my test, nine firms in that industry are "monopolists." The more relevant question surely is not, Can we properly call nine rival firms "monopolies"? but rather, Are there demonstrably better ways to serve consumers? High profit may be the result of dysfunctional monopoly. But it may instead be the consequence of quick response to efficient guides to expansion, economical rewards to innovation, or the best available arrangement where

---

[9]Worcester, "New Estimates of the Welfare Loss to Monopoly," pp. 234–45.

[10]The firms are as follows. The numbers after each name give the number of years of monopoly profit and the number of years among the *Fortune* 500: Kellogg 7/14, Hershey Foods 6/14, Commonwealth Oil 7/10, Texas Gulf 6/6, Reynolds Tobacco 9/14, Minnesota Mining 12/14, Du Pont 10/14, Sterling Drug 9/14, American Home Products 14/14, Briggs and Stratton 8/10, IBM 10/14, Maytag 12/14, Polaroid 7/12, Xerox 8/8, Schering 9/13, Merck 12/14, Eli Lilly 8/14, Parke Davis 6/14, Smith Kline French 14/14, Warner-Lambert 8/14, Upjohn 8/12, Avon Products 14/14, Corning Glass 7/14, Libby-Owens-Ford 7/14, Gillette 14/14, Ingersoll Rand 7/14, Square D 11/14, Champion Spark Plug 12/12, Eastman Kodak 14/14, Brunswick 7/13 (also losses).

economies of scale coexist with supply shortages requiring high prices if the scarce supplies are to be conserved for their more valuable uses.

Just as high profit rates are highly unreliable guides to a wasteful use of resources, low profit rates are a poor guarantee of efficiency. Low, "competitive" profits may exist because valuable resources are dissipated because they are underpriced, or they are used to discourage competition by efficient rivals, perhaps by seeking legislation or favorable rulings. Or dysfunctional high profits may be concealed by writing up assets, especially after purchase, although this does not seem to be done in practice.[11] High profits, especially in smaller businesses, can be transferred to owners in perquisites. Indeed, one must expect accurately measured profit rates to converge toward some uniform level, once risks and the costs of entry are taken into account, *whether or not monopolistic elements continue to exist.* Under ideal circumstances, adjustments that equalize profit rates increase efficiency and serve consumer interests. But profits can be fully dissipated, serving neither efficiency nor consumers. All sources of high incomes—profits from market control, innovation, franchises, tariffs, restrictive practices of trade associations, trade unions, and other devices that bar entry—lead individuals and firms to spend time and money to qualify themselves for "membership." These expenditures plus expenditures by insiders to bar entry to latecomers can be expected to reduce the net retained from higher gross earnings to no more than the insiders and outsiders would get in other occupations or enterprises. If so, no monopoly profits remain, despite the continuing presence of monopolistic restriction and misallocation.

As already noted, this line of reasoning has led Tullock and Posner to include as part of welfare loss the profit used to calculate the Harberger-type welfare loss.[12] Aside from the impossibility of finding, by this procedure, any continuing excess profit or welfare loss once the adjustments are complete, such analysis recognizes no benefits to consumers from efforts to break into and to defend monopoly positions although improved quality, lower prices, better guarantees, and the like are excellent offensive and defensive devices. Comanor

---

[11]Accounting practice disapproves of writing up asset values, and while sales of profitable assets or enterprises could be placed on the books at appreciated values, William W. Alberts does not find the conditions and corporate actions necessary to capitalize profits in the merger activity of the last fifteen years. Hence this particular embarrassment to the measurement of loss monopolistic inefficiency may not hold. See William W. Alberts, "Why Are Welfare Losses from Monopoly Small?" (Paper presented at the Western Economic Association Meetings, San Francisco, June 26, 1976), available from the College of Business Administration, University of Washington, Seattle.

[12]Tullock, "The Welfare Costs of Tariffs, Monopoly and Theft," pp. 224–32; Posner, "The Social Cost of Monopoly and Regulation," pp. 807–29.

and Wilson's approach is much more relevant to welfare loss analysis precisely because it identifies and attempts to measure the extent to which such costs may be dysfunctional without assuming that they are such in their entirety. We have argued that the dysfunctional element is far smaller than that which Comanor and Wilson believe they found. We have pointed out that effectively monopolized industries would operate on a far more elastic section of the industry demand curve than actual industries apparently do. But the immediate point to be made is that low profits are not in themselves a reliable indicator of efficiency.

The difficulty is that the facts of life include indivisibilities, ignorance, moral hazard (the inclination to take personal advantage at the expense of others by sloth, carelessness when insured, and worse), risk-aversion, and the desire for new experiences, for prestige, for influence, and for approval. The costly tools used to accommodate these unruly facts of life are the same ones that stand accused as building blocks of inefficiency: "monopoly" in formal welfare theory. [13]

It should be noted that the continuing presence of monopoly under the circumstances assumed to exist by Tullock and Posner does not result in a worsened distribution of income, either between labor and property income or between different income classes. Increased costs reduce the profit share to competitive rates. The payments for product development and for promotional, legal, and lobbying costs needed to probe for markets and defend against rivals can be expected eventually to absorb all the difference between efficient production costs and price. Because these activities involve the employment of approximately the same range of talents as those involved in efficient physical production, sales, product development, and the like, they will alter slightly if at all the distribution of income among hired personnel.

Price discrimination is often regarded as virtually decisive evidence of inefficiency. But it can also be an efficient accommodation to an indivisibility that does not yield to present-day understanding of nature. Thus monopolistic price discrimination may satisfy consumer wants more efficiently than any feasible alternative economic arrangement whether or not higher than competitive profits are earned. This condition exists when a firm has lower total costs than two or more firms would have producing the same desired total output. It is most likely to happen if the firm is a natural monopoly, that is, has continuously declining average costs throughout the range of output for which demand exists. Such a firm may or may not actually enjoy above average profits even when it practices price discrimination. It is possi-

---

[13]See Harold Demsetz, "Information and Efficiency: Another Viewpoint," *Journal of Law and Economics*, vol. 12 (April 1969), pp. 1–22, for an excellent treatment of this issue.

ble that it will break even only by charging several prices for "the same" product. Perhaps only then can the weighted average of prices equal average costs. But a discriminating monopolist can be highly profitable without attracting entry because two or more firms sharing the market would have higher costs. This celebrated increasing returns case, often used to justify public utility regulation, has recently been reinvestigated. As noted in the discussion of the no-effect theory in Chapter 3, pricing patterns under regulation were found to be similar to the preregulation rate structure with, if anything, more favorable rates to large industrial users and less favorable treatment of smaller users under regulation.[14]

Another undesirable possibility, largely foreclosed in a free market, is opened up by regulation of natural monopolies. Competition may be valued more highly than efficiency by the courts and regulators who together make rival firms profitable by raising charges to consumers (or not reducing them) so as to permit a larger number of firms to exist. The subsidization of entry can engineer an inefficient multifirm industry where a natural monopoly would save resource costs and serve consumers better.[15]

This discussion can be summarized by noting that it is closely related to barriers to entry. Natural monopolies, protected by economies of scale, may be revealed by high profits, although profitless natural monopolies can exist. High cost barriers can be inferred from certain types of expenses needed to penetrate or manipulate markets or to resist their penetration and manipulation by rivals. Either way, one expects to find relatively few sellers, that is, high concentration ratios. These are easy to discover by simple statistical techniques. It is not surprising, therefore, that concentration and "fewness" have come to signal, virtually to serve as surrogates for, barriers, inefficiency, and monopoly. Economists and lawyers who have achieved high stations have gone so far as to recommend high concentration as presumptive evidence of collusion.[16] Firms would be called upon to overcome a presumption of guilt! Guilty they would be unless they could prove their innocence beyond a reasonable doubt.[17] If this is accepted in law, all difficulties involved in discovering marginal costs

---

[14]See Jordan, "Producer Protection," pp. 151–52 and references cited there.

[15]This seems to be one issue in the case against the Bell system. Similar logic figured in the decision against The Atlantic and Pacific Tea Company.

[16]For example, see Kaysen and Turner, *Antitrust Policy, an Economic and Legal Analysis,* for an early but still influential statement.

[17]This inversion of the constitutional guarantees is already the fact in many cases. Warrantless searches that would be cause for dismissal of charges in criminal prosecutions are routine procedures by the Federal Trade Commission and the Occupational Safety and Health Administration.

and prices, all the problems that must be solved if monopoly profits are to be separated from functionally desirable profits that finance useful expenditures for innovation and valuable information for consumers, all the frustrations involved in distinguishing natural from contrived monopoly will be bypassed. Expanded regulation can proceed without regard to costs and benefits. But there is no reason to expect benefits for consumers to result from this activism.

Concentration Ratios as Indicators of Monopoly

The concentration ratio is usually the percentage of sales produced by the four or eight largest firms. Firms are presumed by some investigators to collude or somehow to coordinate their policies to achieve monopoly profits if only four, or eight, produce a large share of the industry output.

The presumptive case for linking high concentration ratios with monopoly rests on a theory of collusion that centers on price-matching. In a formal model, when firms meticulously match prices, raising and lowering them simultaneously by the same amount, each firm will tend to get its share of sales.[18] This makes the elasticity of demand of each firm the same as the elasticity of demand for the industry as a whole, and it makes the firm's best profit position one where marginal cost is below price. This is the formal test for monopoly stated at the beginning of this chapter. This could happen if firms made and stuck to a collusive agreement always to follow the prices set by a price leader, or simply watched each other closely and matched any price change instituted by any firm in the industry. The main difficulties with this theory are that it does not fit the known facts about elasticities of demand and the hypothesis that firms try to enlarge their profits. One might think that such difficulties would relegate the theory to the scrap heap, but the theory survives.

If firms did collude, their elasticities of demand would be the same as the elasticities for their industries. The data on elasticities sum-

---

[18]Some readers will wonder why this is not true no matter how many firms may serve a market. After all, in that case a single price is expected to prevail in the market and all firms will accept the prices they find on the market and will tend to get their share of sales. The difference lies in the fact that with many sellers it is not possible, or not worthwhile, to keep track of so many rivals. Thus any firm that intentionally lets its price drop just a little will draw off some customers from so many rivals that it cannot serve them all. Likewise, it will lose a few customers to each of many rivals if its prices get a bit too high. This "cross elasticity" makes its effective demand curve very much flatter, "more elastic," than its industry share curve. The same phenomenon exists when firms are few, but it is less prominent and is often given less weight than it deserves. See Yale Brozen, "The Antitrust Task Force Deconcentration Recommendation," *Journal of Law and Economics*, vol. 13 (October 1970).

marized in Chapter 3, which includes virtually all that could be found in the literature, suggest that most demand curves are inelastic (between -1.0 and 0.0) or not very elastic (between -2.0 and -1.0), with very few as elastic as -3.0. If firms had demand curves like these and were to maximize their profits, their prices would be very much higher than their marginal costs. For example, many industries—including petroleum, steel, and automobiles—have inelastic demands. Thus if the hypothesis connecting high concentration ratios to monopoly power were true, so that firms had the same elasticity as their industries, the firms could greatly increase their total revenues if they sold a lesser amount at a higher price. They would, of course, in addition, save some costs by producing less. These findings simply contradict the belief that firms in these industries collude and maximize their profits. Another way to state it is to note that if the collusion theory is correct, they must have colluded not to increase their profits but rather to carry production far beyond the point that would give them their highest return and well into the level where additional production *lowers* their *total* return from sales.

Since marginal cost cannot be as low as zero, and even less can it be below zero (as is required for maximization if elasticities lie between 0.0 and -1.0), elasticities of -1.0 and less imply a degree of competition that has expanded output beyond the level that maximizes industry profits. Equally suggestive of efficiency is the fact that profit rates in concentrated industries differ little from profit rates in unconcentrated industries although profit margins would be much higher if concentration enables firms to bring their individual demand curves closer to the low elasticity of market share curve. The conspicuous absence of all steel and automobile firms from the list of firms earning more than 5 percent "monopoly" profits for as few as six of fourteen years is only one of many studies that supports this result.[19]

One short-run hypothesis that attempts to account for these facts is essentially political, and it is passed over lightly here because it is inferior on the principle of Occam's razor. This short-run hypothesis is that the firms have monopoly power but choose not to use it. It is inferior because it rests on subjective factors scarcely capable of objective refutation. A superior hypothesis recognizes real limitations on each firm's range of choices even when few rivals are present.

Suppose there are only a few firms of equal size in a market and that although they see advantages in colluding, they also perceive risks if some of the others back out of the agreement. They may, in addition, have reason to expect additional rivals to appear who will not be party

---

[19]See footnote 10, above, and also, for example, Brozen, "The Antitrust Task Force Deconcentration Recommendation."

to any agreement, but that expectation is ignored for the moment. Each firm knows that if it raises its price, some customers will be lost to the other firms. The number lost will depend in part upon the ability of the others to produce more and in part upon the sensitivity of its present customers to the price change. If customers are very sensitive, they will all try to go, but unless the rivals can supply them, they will have to choose between being supplied at the higher price or going without. It follows that if the rivals can sell quite a lot more without running into higher costs (which is to say that their supply curves are "elastic"), the price-raising firm will eventually lose many customers, far more than if all firms raised their prices together. If they all raised together, only those who would rather go without would be lost; each firm would lose only its share. But each would lose some. So each firm's share of the industry demand also affects the firm's demand curve.

These three things—elasticity of industry demand, elasticity of rivals' supply curves, and the firm's share of the industry demand—have a surprisingly large effect on the elasticity of demand for a firm. For example, the second largest oil company in the United States produces about 5 percent of U.S. oil. (The largest produces about 10 percent.) If the industry demand curve is, as estimated, the "inelastic" -0.46, and the other firms have the very inelastic supply elasticity of only 0.25, the firm's elasticity comes out at -13.95. This means that a one percent price increase will reduce sales by 13.95 percent. An elasticity of supply of 1.0 is probably more nearly correct, and, if so, the firm's elasticity is -28.2.

The equation that yields this result is

$$E_f = \frac{1}{S}E_d - (\frac{1}{S}-1)E_s$$

where E_f is the elasticity of demand for a firm's output, S is its fractional share of the market, E_d is the elasticity of the industry demand curve (which carries a negative sign since the curve is downward sloping), and E_s is the elasticity of supply from the other firms in the industry (with a positive sign since the curve is upward sloping). In the absence of agreement, or government regulation to ensure "fairness" or "equal treatment" of rivals, this formula expresses some of the facts of the market to which the firms must adjust. One very important fact that is left out of account is the possible impact of *potential* rivals either of the same or foreign nationality. Even without this threat, the constraint felt by a firm with as much as a third of its market may be substantial. In an industry with a demand elasticity of -1.0, and a supply elasticity of 2.0, it will find itself with an elasticity of -7.0. This implies a profit-maximizing price 16.7 percent above marginal cost. But smaller rivals have higher elasticities (because the S in their equation is smaller) and will think a lower price is their profit-maximizing price. Then too, the higher the price is, the more likely it is to turn potential competition into real competition, perhaps in the form of a major expansion by some well-organized large firm with some reason to think that it has discovered a way to get a competitive edge.

The profit-maximizing monopoly markup can be calculated for any elasticity of demand. The markup is, of course, price minus marginal cost divided by marginal cost. Profits are maximized when marginal cost is equal to marginal revenue because the former tells how much is added to the firm's total costs and the latter how much is added to its total revenues by producing and selling one unit more. Marginal revenue is given by $M = P(1 + \frac{1}{E_f})$, where M is marginal revenue (set equal to marginal cost if profits are maximized), P is price (set equal to 1.0 for convenience), and E_f is the firm's elasticity of demand. As stated in the preceding paragraph, if the demand elasticity for the firm is -7.0, the markup that maximizes profits is 16.7 percent above marginal cost; if elasticity is 28.2, the *profit-maximizing* markup is 3.68 percent—on the assumption that the other smaller firms do not set what appears to them to be their (lower) profit-maximizing prices and that the prices set do not result in profits high enough to attract entry by other firms.

One must make some assumptions to get an idea of what an industrywide profit-maximizing price would be like if firms could monopolize their markets, because the nature of the demand elasticity at prices greatly different than past *(relative)* prices is unknown. But assume that the demand curve is a straight line, so that elasticity and marginal revenue rise in a predictable way as output falls. This is reasonable because at higher prices the range of substitutes widens. Taking the oil industry's demand elasticity of $-.46$ as an example, and assuming an arbitrarily chosen price of $1 per unit of output to simplify the calculation, by applying the equation given in the preceding paragraph, each additional unit of output *reduces* total receipts by $1.1739, as shown in Figure 4 when marginal revenue is *minus* $1.1739. Profits would be maximized if output were reduced until marginal revenue is equal to marginal cost, here assumed to be equal to price, or $1.

If one were to assume (as some apparently do) that it costs nothing at all to produce petroleum and its products, marginal revenue would equal a zero marginal cost and profit maximization would require a reduction of output to 73 percent of the current level (see Figure 4). A price of about $1.59 would reduce sales that much. (See the point, in Figure 4, on the demand curve above the output where the marginal revenue line crosses the quantity axis.)

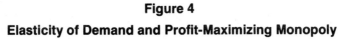

Figure 4

Elasticity of Demand and Profit-Maximizing Monopoly

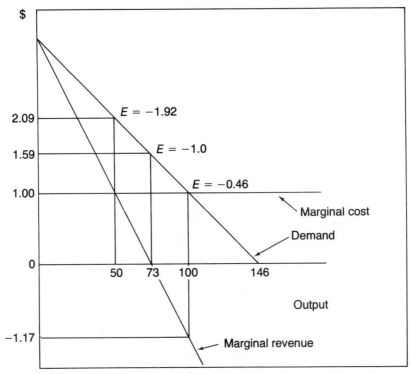

Profit maximization, however, involves a reduction to half the current output according to the demand curve assumed in this example. This brings us up the marginal revenue line high enough to meet marginal costs and brings the elasticity of demand to −1.92. If, as Department of Energy publicists insist on inferring in the face of massive knowledge to the contrary, demand remains inelastic at higher prices, it is all the more wonder that the oil companies should have failed to find a way to restrict output so as to improve their profits. The power of competition seems to be powerful indeed, and it can only be increased by the present highly touted energy shortage and the drive to develop additional sources of power. It can be expected to increase the availability of substitutes, rotating and flattening the industry demand for oil and increasing its elasticity.

It is no wonder that firms in industries with rivals tend eventually to agree to go along with regulation by government that will limit imports, stabilize their share of the market at "fair" prices, limit the

91

entry of rival firms and new products, and perhaps also delay or prohibit the introduction of new cost-cutting processes by rivals.

It has already been noted that longer-run considerations limit the ability and inclination of firms tempted to collude, quite in the absence of threats of legal action by the Department of Justice or the Federal Trade Commission. Entry is invited when profit margins are large if unsatisfied demand can be developed at lower prices. A helpful way to view the problem confronting a firm with some current monopoly power is from the vantage point of a new product. Every new product is, initially, a monopoly. What marketing strategy is the best? Three strategies have been suggested. One strategy is to set a monopolistic price and collude with rivals when they appear—colluding on prices and sharing of the market. This is an example of the just discussed collusive strategy.

A second strategy is to enter big, "filling the market" to such an extent that potential rivals will expect such low returns that they will not enter. This is called a "limit price" strategy. If the collusive strategy is followed, one would expect to find firms of approximately equal size in the market. This is a testable hypothesis. In the United States, a preponderance of antitrust and related cases have in fact been filed against such firms. If the limit price strategy is followed, one would expect to find one firm that is very much bigger than the others, if, indeed, there were any rivals at all. This is also testable.

A third strategy is possible. It is to price so as to get excellent short-run profits, recognizing that rivals will be attracted. When they appear, instead of reducing output and sharing the market, so as to hold price to the monopoly level, the lead firm maintains, perhaps expands, production if the total market is growing. This forces the new firm to set lower prices if it is to find a market. At that time, the original firm matches the lower prices set by the new rival so as to maintain his output. This can be called a quantity-leadership : price-followership or "independent maximization" strategy. If followed, it will tend to produce a pattern of firm sizes where the largest firm is about twice the size of the next largest, the second about twice the size of the third largest, and so on, provided that all firms have similar costs and the spacing in time is uniform. This is also a testable hypothesis, and has been tested.[20]

All three hypotheses relate to products, not firms, since most firms produce many products that have been introduced at different times. Data by product are in any case much more relevant to monopoly than broad industry data usually used in studies of monopoly.

[20]Dean A. Worcester, Jr., *Monopoly, Big Business and Welfare in Postwar United States* (Seattle: University of Washington Press, 1967), pp. 87–97.

This author investigated relative product concentration using a sample of five-digit and seven-digit product data for U.S. manufacturing industries. These data are far more detailed than the data used in most studies, and in particular, far more detailed than those for the forty-one industries used by Comanor and Wilson. There are about 1,000 (five-digit Standard Industrial Classification) categories, which are subdivided more finely into about 7,000 (seven-digit) subcategories in the universe from which my sample was drawn. I found a preponderance conforming to the quantity-leadership expectation.[21]

An obvious implication of the quantity-leadership: price-followership or independent maximization hypothesis is that entry will continue until the rate of profit is equal to that in other industries—the equalization of profit theorem that goes back at least to Ricardo and implies essentially competitive markets. This theorem holds even if relatively few firms actually exist in a market and the leading firms continue to produce 50 percent or more of the industry output. The a priori expectation is for a very wide dispersion of firm sizes of the order 52 percent, 26 percent, 13 percent, 6 percent, 3 percent shares of the market with only five firms. It is consistent with the actual profit rates observed in industry and with the low elasticities of industry demand found in concentrated markets. Monopoly theories are inconsistent with all these.

The independent maximization hypothesis assumes that all firms have about the same average and marginal costs. Comanor and Wilson's statistical analysis, and that of other investigators, is inconsistent with that assumption. They find the larger firms to have *lower* average costs. One must expect, therefore, either that very few small firms should have continued to exist or that they will soon cease to exist since they can merge into firms that are large enough to achieve more efficient scale. Yet "inefficient-sized" firms persist for decades in many industries.

Any of several conditions, each of which implies an efficient use of resources, may account for this phenomenon. Alfred Marshall would probably think in terms of a life cycle of firms, with younger and obsolescent firms being smaller and having low profits. A closer look at individual industries may show differences of location and product specialties that account for differences in relative size and apparent profitability. There are surely significant differences of capability of management that tend to locate the most able in the larger enterprises where they manage more resources. To the extent that managers and owner-managers receive their income from profits, the lower returns to the less able managers may still be more than they can get in other

---

[21]Ibid., chap. 6, especially Tables V1-2, V1-3, and V1-4, pp. 111–13.

lines of work. If so, costs are economically no higher than in the larger firms. The apparent high cost of the smaller firms is reflective of a lower quality of management, which is efficiently allocated among relevant alternatives. This last point is underscored by the common practice of smaller firms, which are more nearly the property of the owners and therefore can be used to pay out what amounts to tax-free salaries in the form of perquisites that appear on the firm's books as costs.

In any case, the incidence of high concentration and widely disparate firm size in product markets defined narrowly enough to exclude many noncompeting goods is very much higher than usually reported.[22] Nevertheless, the performance of the economy seems to be very much closer to desirable performance, competitive performance, than the degree of adherence to the formal criteria for competition apparently implies to some investigators. It seems clear that high concentration ratios do not permit a direct inference either of efficiency or inefficiency, but that superior efficiency by firms acting independently is at least as likely an explanation of high concentration as is monopolistic collusion. Nor have consumer interests suffered.

Summary

Formal economic models associate monopoly with inefficiency. Less formal models have associated monopoly with income distributions skewed in favor of profits at the expense of labor incomes and in favor of high incomes at the expense of low incomes. None of these associations is necessarily valid. Market structures that meet the usual criteria for competition are sometimes inefficient and contribute to an unequal distribution of income. Others that seem to fulfill the conditions for monopoly set out by formal theory sometimes, perhaps typically, come rather close to efficient outputs and competitive distribution.

The problem lies in the fact that the conditions postulated in the formal model, although extremely useful for positive economics, are not useful for normative theory and policy analysis because very important facts in the real world, properly ignored or held constant when formulating and testing hypotheses that enhance understanding, can neither be ignored nor held constant when choosing among alternative policies or economic structures that must deal with these facts.

Relative profit rates and concentration ratios are popular indirect indicators of monopoly power. Both turn out to be unreliable tests of efficiency. Monopolistic market strategies fit the combination of exist-

---

[22]Ibid., chap. 4.

ing high levels of concentration, elasticities, and dispersion of firm sizes less well than an independent maximization or quantity-leadership: price-followership strategy that leads industries to approximately competitive performance despite high concentration ratios and large differences in firm size. This chapter is critical of the economic analysis that has informed government policy for the last forty years. The next chapter attempts to construct a normative theory that can be useful for policy makers.

5

Toward a
Normative Economic Theory
Suitable for Policy Choices

This chapter brings together several bodies of analysis. The objective is to develop a theoretical model suitable for normative analysis. Two major elements are essential to the task: (1) inclusion of dimensions for all the unavoidable realities such as the geographical dispersion of consumers and productive agents, consumer ignorance of the cost and the characteristics of goods, and the potential that regulation has to increase monopoly control; and (2) a distinction between scarcity rents, which increase toward a maximum when resources are used more efficiently, and profits, which direct change but diminish toward zero as desirable change is completed, except under monopoly. These principles are then applied to several issues related to advertising.

Theorizing based on rivalry among firms and individuals is more appropriate for policy than the standard competitive model that assumes individuals and firms to be, ideally, without influence in any market, or elsewhere. But more is needed for a normative theory. The key elements are, perhaps, approached by dividing factor earnings between what can best be thought of as rents and profits.

Rivalry[1] is traditionally associated with imperfect markets where each decision maker needs to take into consideration the choices made by others. Decisions are not just a matter of responding to market prices, but also anticipating the prices, quality changes, advertising campaigns, and other activities that may affect sales. This complicates mathematical manipulation and introduces an unwelcome degree of uncertainty into the model by requiring knowledge of just how one person's actions are affected by his guess about what others will do. In principle, "oligopolistic uncertainty," the technical name for this effect of rivalry, makes anything possible a priori, thereby yielding soft-

---

[1]Schumpeter, *Capitalism, Socialism and Democracy*, uses the term "creative destruction" to carry much the same meaning. See especially chaps. 6–8.

edged rather than hard-edged hypotheses for testing. Theory based on rivalry, therefore, is weaker than traditional competitive theory as a discoverer of relationships.

The simplifications, useful for discovery, are damaging for policy-oriented theory because policy must not neglect real differences that can properly be neglected or held constant by assumption when the objective is different. For example, it is not helpful when considering institutional change to think in terms of homogeneous supplies of factors and products, all existing at the same geographical location with time to make adjustments and with information in free supply, although it is often helpful to do so when formulating testable hypotheses that yield knowledge. Indeed, knowledge is obtained by observing deviations from expectations based on the model. Nor does it improve analysis for policy purposes to think of firms as if each were a unit identical to an indefinitely large number in its particular line of production, all of them, ideally, having a very small list of options: produce more or less at a given price; introduce a new product just like others already on the market; passively accept the present structure of laws, regulations, and types of contractual arrangements; feel no pressure from others or any need to attempt to change others' points of view by persuasion or the force of law; do not investigate other parameters of possible action. Joseph Schumpeter described this model of competition as "barely alive," and "like Hamlet without the Danish prince."[2]

A theory of rivalry views individuals as well as firms as heads-up decision makers looking in all directions for better opportunities and allocating themselves from one activity to another rather than making small adjustments of more or less. In this they act more like the traditional landowner deciding whether to plow or rent, whether to put the west forty into wheat, oats, or corn, so as to maximize the return from his "fixed factor," his farm. In that sense, *every* factor owner, whether the asset is personal ability, a physical good, or plot of land, willy-nilly makes decisions on how his or her resources are to be used and in return gets an income that is like a "rent" to a "fixed factor" called here "factor rents."

Recognition of "real-life" constraints leaves a crucial roadblock to rational policy making still in place. At least one writer is explicit about the problem. Steven N. S. Cheung writes,

> Thus the world is inefficient only when the system chosen to analyze it fails to specify the gains and costs of every action described. . . . Inasmuch as we have ignored the constraints

---

[2]Ibid., pp. 77, 86.

binding legislative decision making, the implied solution in our analysis of price control falls short of satisfying the Pareto condition.[3]

Cheung's conclusion is unavoidable. If *all* constraints on *everyone's* activities are taken fully into account, only one outcome is possible, and in a sense it is efficient.

The idea of normative theory is troublesome because it introduces complexity and value judgments. Normative analysis cannot assume that the conditions held constant or abstracted from in conventional analysis will not materially frustrate attainment of the desired outcomes when constraints are changed by the introduction of regulation. So the number of variables explicitly considered must be more numerous. But inclusion of these variables results only in a higher level of positive analysis as long as no judgment is made about which of various realistically possible states of the economy is the better.

A suitable analogy to complex positive analysis is the study of weather so as to predict but not to modify actual weather on specific days. Normative activity involves such things as cloud-seeding and shelter-belts intended to improve the weather. Normative analysis in economics begins when changed outcomes are sought by changing the starting points from which individual and firm activity begin, or the legal and regulatory structure is altered in ways that expand or limit the choices one may make. When this is done, criteria are needed to measure the *desirability* of alternative outcomes.

A Broader Scope Is Needed

Among the conditions which are held constant by conventional positive economics, and which rational policy making needs to treat as variables when regulating advertising, are the following: product characteristics; the possibilities of using government regulation to organize a monopoly; the consequences of increased credulity of buyers when statements about safety, effectiveness, and quality of goods are certified by government; and the effects on the credibility of government itself and thus its effectiveness when it undertakes such activities. Several of these variables already have been examined on an ad hoc basis. A broadening of perspective is needed even within the purely market arena. For example, the costs of dealing with geographically dispersed customers and resources cannot be assumed away, as they usually are in economic studies, but rather they must be recognized and dealt with.

---

[3]Cheung, "A Theory of Price Control," p. 71.

Adding all relevant variables will not automatically lead to a basis for regulation and reform. A choice among possible outcomes must be made. But in a society where the government is responsive to pressures from individuals and organized groups, improved understanding of cause and effect relationships in these areas may help harmonize efforts to change the system of constraints when net gains to all affected groups are possible. Private contracting, lobbying for new legislation or the repeal of existing laws, attempts to change present regulations, bringing legal suits, and similar efforts to change legal constraints by private actions need to be included in normative analysis as a major part of the goal-setting process. But even if government or some other source of exogenous "moral" authority can dominate outcomes from "above the battle," more than knowledge of cause and effect is required to evaluate policies. Evaluation requires a norm, a basis for selecting the better from alternatives that can exist.

The technique of normative economics proposed here resembles the familiar one of efficiency or Pareto optimality, in which individuals starting with given endowments interact until some point on a "contract curve" is reached where no one can gain without making someone else worse off. In nearly every case, both parties gain when compared with the starting point. What is at issue here is the effect of changed *legal constraints* and *regulation* that shifts the *starting points* from which exchange takes place. Altering legal constraints can be a form of contracting that sets mutually more advantageous rules. The normative problem is to determine which starting point is the *most desirable* for the participants. Altered starting points may result in higher values for all parties whether or not subsequent exchange more closely approaches the conditions laid down by formal welfare economics.[4]

The shift can, in principle, have any of three general effects. It may only redistribute wealth or rights, leaving the total unchanged. It may alter them in such a way as to increase their aggregate value. Or it may alter them in such a way as to destroy or dissipate some values. If values are increased, the change produces a net gain to resource owners, which can be called a "factor rent," along with increased efficiency of resource use. If aggregate value is decreased, "factor profits" in some sectors accompany a larger reduction of values, "factor losses" in other sectors. There is a decline of efficiency and a reduction or dissipation of aggregate rents. If aggregate value is unaffected, the change is a "transfer" with offsetting "profits" and "losses"

---

[4]This is true because the gain from the larger "pie" can be greater than the loss from its less efficient division. See Schumpeter, *Capitalism, Socialism and Democracy*, p. 106; McGee, *In Defense of Industrial Concentration*, pp. 75–79; and Sam Peltzman, "The Gains and Losses from Industrial Concentration."

to resource owners. Transfers without consequences for efficiency are unlikely to be encountered in reality, so attention is focused on the distinction between factor rent at equilibrium and long-term factor (monopoly) profit. Some clues are investigated that help to distinguish between the two in practical situations.

Both rent and profit carry negative connotations to many, perhaps most, voters, but profit would probably be regarded as more socially valuable than rent. It is therefore necessary to define and analyze the reality referred to with these terms. The first will be profits.

Profit has always carried two major meanings: return to management, innovation, and risk-taking—to entrepreneurship—on one hand, and return in excess of cost—to privilege—on the other. Since important, costly social functions are performed by entrepreneurs, the first kind of profit is better conceived as a return for human effort, a wage. It fluctuates widely with the fortunes of an enterprise since it is what is left after the hired personnel and purchased supplies receive their more stable contracted returns. But profits of this type must be received if the function is to be performed, so they are a part of cost. Profits in the sense of a return to privilege—monopoly profits—flow to those who find ways to restrict production. It is a privilege that may be obtained primarily by exercising the same entrepreneurial functions that have desirable outcomes in the absence of privilege. But the arrangements that permit restriction, commonly called "monopoly," reduce efficiency. A basic problem of economic organization is to improve social arrangements so as to improve opportunities to earn rewards for management, innovation, and assumption of risk while reducing the opportunities to earn monopoly profit.

The problem of rent is conceptually the reverse of the problem of monopoly profit. Higher factor rents accompany increased efficiency. Recently, economists have again become keenly interested in the need for appropriate rents if resources are to be put to their best uses. Since this point conflicts with common sense, the basic argument and an example are given in the next section.[5]

Rent as Factor Rent: The Problem of Government Regulation

The meanings assigned to the terms rent and profit differ enough from writer to writer and (with modifiers) refer to such different things as to

---

[5]For a more complete analysis that generalizes this relationship, see Dean A. Worcester, Jr., "Technological and Pecuniary Externality: Factor Rents and Social Costs," *American Economic Review*, vol. 59 (December 1969), especially pp. 873–80.

make it necessary to clarify the meanings assigned here.[6] In the present context rents are to be distinguished from "economic" rents (the amount by which the payment to a factor, or agent, of production exceeds the amount needed to keep it at its present task), from rent as the payment for the use of a natural resource and, of course, from profit. As used here, rent is the return to a property right. This is a very broad usage since each individual has property rights in his own labor as well as any other valuable resources that he may own. Yet from the point of view of the individual, the economic problem is exactly to deploy his ownership rights, specifically including his personal activities, in such a way as to make his property right as valuable to himself as he can. He may work for himself or rent himself out on the best terms available. He may be able to improve his value by investing in self-improvement or he can decide to live on his "capital" in riotous living. In something close to the classical sense, each person who is not a slave has a fixed supply of potential talent given by nature that can be consumed or augmented in much the same way that an owner of a plot of land can use the land. This usage is consistent with the geographical dispersion and differences in capabilities, age, and desires that characterize the real world of activity, recognized by Hayek as an unavoidable aspect of the "problem of economics," a problem that is almost totally ignored by the formal model found unsuitable for normative purposes in Chapter 4.[7]

Viewed this way, social arrangements that increase the net factor rents increase social values. These are in turn derived from deploying the rent-yielding assets in such a way as to render increased value to those who contract for their use—in the last analysis the final consumers of the outputs of the assets.

One of the many paradoxes in economics is the teaching that if some units of a scarce resource are not owned, or are owned by a person or group that fails to charge as much as can be charged for its

---

[6]The basic idea that distinguishes rent from other returns is the irrelevance of the size of its renumeration to the existence of the productive resource. Just what is meant by the existence of a resource is muddled. To Ricardo it was the continued presence of the original and indestructible nature of abstract "land." "Economic rents," by contrast, are earned by any productive resource receiving a higher return in its present use than needed to hold it there, "existence" in the sense of staying at its present task. "Monopoly rents" are returns to owners of enterprises in excess of their opportunity costs, again more than that needed to keep them at their present tasks, something that in this case implies a smaller than socially optimal productive effort, not compensated by fully increased output elsewhere. In general, it is necessary to accompany the word "rent" with an adjective and perhaps a sentence or two of definition if one hopes to be understood. In these circumstances the wiser course might be to abandon use of the term, but understanding is enhanced by working out the essential ideas with reference to familiar modes of thought and analogous uses of some familiar terminology.

[7]Hayek, "The Price System as a Mechanism for Using Knowledge."

102

use, the value of *other* assets is *reduced*. Put another way, the value of other assets is dissipated because they are wastefully deployed in the absence of an accurate guide to the appropriate intensity of use of the unowned and therefore free or underpriced scarce resource. Fished out lakes, polluted air, despoiled public parks, illustrate the phenomena.

Figure 5

The Productivity of Rent

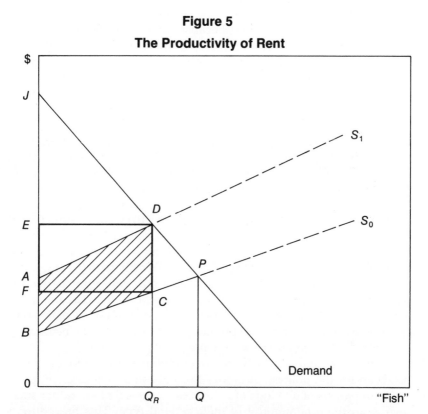

Note: S_0 represents social costs for alternative outputs under two conditions: (1) when the resource is newly discovered, and (2) when it is used efficiently over the long term. The latter requires reduction of overuse, which can be accomplished by a rental charge. In practice, the curves relevant to these two situations will differ, but both lie significantly below the social costs of inefficient use caused by wasteful overuse of the resource. S_1 also represents costs under two conditions: (1) real costs when overuse of the resource is permitted, and (2) money cost when resources useful in the production of other goods and services are used efficiently, and "land" is priced (or otherwise restricted) so as to prevent overuse. Again, these two curves need not be identical, as they are here, but both will lie above S_0. In any case, the price to the consumer is higher, $0E$ rather than $0F$, because it is necessary to allocate, or to ration, the available supply Q_R among competitive uses. If the good is not rationed explicitly by price, it will be rationed by other means that are no less costly to consumers.

A simple geometrical figure may help a doubting reader understand why this is so. Line BS_0 in Figure 5 indicates the alternative opportunity costs of attracting additional individuals and firms into enterprises that produce "fish." At present, it is assumed, the "fishery" has just been discovered and no arrangement that would put a value on the fishery itself has been conceived that would not cost more than it seems to be worth. Therefore, the fishery can be used without charge. Before long, a peak output of Q is reached, and the typical price received is P. Then, because of intensive use, the catch per fisherman declines, lowering return per unit of investment, total output, and raising the cost per fish caught. In time, price rises to point D as quantity stabilizes at Q_R. Before depletion, Q_R could be caught annually with a resource cost of $B0Q_RC$. After depletion, the annual cost of the same quantity is $A0Q_RD$. If depletion is forestalled, price C yields as big an income to each of the fewer people as price D does to the larger number. But price D is a true scarcity price because output cannot continue at a higher level than Q_R with presently known technology. Failure to charge price D simply diverts some resources from places where they might have done something of value into this industry where they add nothing at all. The shaded area $ABCD$ indicates the annual value of the wasted effort. This is a net reduction of "factor rents." Capitalizing, it gives the lost value of assets.

Some arrangement that limits fishing to the most efficient methods, and the total catch to Q_R, would be worth up to the amount of otherwise wasted resources. An arrangement would not be worthwhile if it cost more to think up, install, and enforce than the amount of waste avoided. Finding ways to discover where economies of this type are possible and getting them put into effect efficiently can be thought of as the *problem of government regulation.*

The traditional way Western governments have sought efficiency has been for the political authority to establish and enforce property rights in parcels of all kinds of resources, parcels that are rather small relative to the total amount of their general type. This procedure is relatively cheap, tends to put every parcel in the hands of someone who is on the lookout for a more valuable use for it, and avoids the wastes of monopoly. All Western nations have followed this practice for manpower by reducing the unit of ownership down to the individual. In free societies each individual deploys his or her own labor among alternatives that he or she is able to discover. This method is also used for capital goods and land in most instances, although public and private nonowners have increasingly acquired managerial responsibility. The social function served by ownership is exactly the deployment of resources to their most valuable uses. This inevitably carries the right to withhold the asset from less valuable uses so, from a negative point of view, it is as exclusionary as it is a charter of opportunity from a positive point of view. Whatever agency, enterprise, or person has the right to deploy a given parcel of resources exercises ownership right. The parcel of resources can be, to repeat, a given person's labor, a house, a factory, an acre of land, or any other asset of value. Absence of ownership rights or failure wisely to define and enforce public or private ownership functions results in lower aggregate asset values.

The value of each parcel of labor, house, or whatever depends upon knowledge of the value of alternative uses to which it might be put. Information, advertising in a broad sense, is essential for this purpose. It is a valuable part of the productive process. Hence, some labor and other resources maximize their values by devoting part of their efforts to advertising their capabilities, thereby increasing the factor rents of others as well. Just what amount of resources is best deployed in this way and just how they can best be used is part of the problem of efficiency, but it is evident that it is possible to devote too little as well as too much to the task. Government action can be corrective, but it can also demand excessive amounts of information, driving costs up more than benefits, or place restrictions on information that reduce knowledge and result in poor choices.

Distributional effects complicate the process of implementing arrangements that would otherwise reduce the intensity of resource use to efficient levels. The supply curves drawn in Figure 5 illustrate an easily overlooked aspect of the problem of regulation. There an owner that forced the more efficient productive method and intensity by charging the maximum rent EFCD (outlined with a heavy line) would earn that amount less any collection costs. The gross revenue is, in this instance, larger than the saving from more efficient production (the difference between the heavily outlined rent area and the value of increased production, the shaded area ABCD). So although the total assets of society are greater, the increased income of the person who obtained ownership of the fishery is larger than the total saving, leaving the others worse off. In this case there is a conflict between the gains from improved institutional arrangements obtained by granting unfettered private rights and the Pareto criterion as usually understood—that no one suffer loss as a result of recontracting.

A representative democracy can be thought of as extending contracting to the formation of laws and regulations that alter the rights of action, the starting points, of its citizens. Such a government would not establish a right that would produce an income for the right-holder large enough to purchase the total output of the resources reallocated to more productive uses and more besides. The factual situation that produces the conditions illustrated by Figure 5 does not preclude improvement of efficiency, because an appropriately limited property right can benefit all parties. Part of the problem of government regulation is to find ways to increase the total assets of members of society. Another part is to find acceptable ways to share the increase while encouraging persistent search for additional improvements. The distributional constraint on efficiency applies as cogently to public ownership as it does to private ownership.

Total rents can be reduced in three ways: by failing to establish rights that permit charges to users equal to the scarcity value of the resource, by prohibiting or limiting valuable uses, and by establishing rights that permit one party to gain while imposing larger costs on others. The former leads to wasteful overuse and diversion of too many complementary resources into what is in effect a subsidized use. The second results in underuse and the diversion of complementary resources into lower-valued activities. The last named is the traditional basis for private monopoly. It is the base for "factor profit," which is quite different from rent.

Factor Profit

The proviso that the parcel of resource owned by an individual be small enough relative to the total is important, whatever the resource—land, capital, enterprise, or labor. A single managerial decision maker able to control too much of the output of a class of production will be able to get an exceptional monopoly reward that will reduce the total value of cooperating assets rather than increase them. This is a particularly important problem because there is no difference between the objective sought (an increased value of one's assets) or the legal and appropriate way to proceed (offer information, advertise, seek information about needs people have and alternative ways to satisfy them, contract with others, seek changes in laws and regulations, bring suit for damages) that distinguishes socially valuable increases in assets, here called "rent-creation," from socially harmful reduction in the value of assets, here called "profit-creation." In both cases the individual is simply searching out the most valuable alternative use of the resources under his control. Reliance on "moral restraint" is for that reason hopeless. Nor is the opinion of this or that "moral leader" in either public or private life likely to have any significant effect, because, to those involved, the leader always (often correctly) appears to be uninformed or to be speaking for a special interest group that has acquired some questionable favor.

The long-term consequence of having "too large" a parcel is illus-

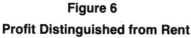

Figure 6
Profit Distinguished from Rent

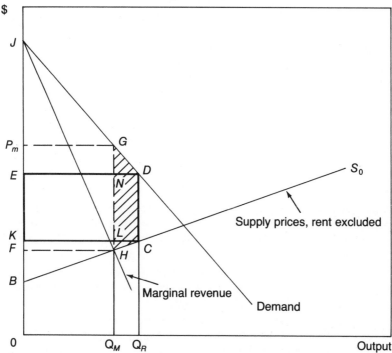

trated in Figure 6. It illustrates the extreme case where the output of the whole industry is controlled by the owner of one of the essential elements of production. It may be exclusive control of one of the natural resources used, of a unit of indispensable machinery, of one or more of the types of labor needed, or something else. The maximum value obtainable by the resources retaining employment in this industry (if only one price is charged) comes with an output of O_M. Whoever has control will, if possible, use efficient techniques so as to hold the amount of work and payments to others to a minimum and so increase the net as much as possible. Opportunity costs will be like those shown as BS_o in Figure 5; the rent plus excess return will be the large (dashed line) rectangle P_mFHG of which $EKLN$ is rent (down by $NLCD$) and the rest is monopoly profit. Any resource owner can in principle capture the whole amount of his rent plus profit if he can control the output of the whole industry. The owner will try to increase the value of his assets so the waste involved in the overuse of unpriced resources is avoided, but losses occur in the opposite direction. Too few of the assets of all the others outside this industry are used. Their value can be increased by reducing the amount of the industry output under control of a single owner.

The previous discussion of the deadweight social loss to monopoly is relevant here. Remembering that price D and rent DC per unit is needed to prevent waste, the total loss is shown by the shaded area $GHCD$ in Figure 6. More exactly it is the capitalized value of the income shown by this area. It consists of loss of net values to individuals as consumers, GND; of net value to individuals as producers in the industry, LHC; and the loss of values of the assets specific to the industry, the rents $NLCD$. The transfers that do not affect the total asset values of the society, but were gained by monopoly, are the rectangular areas P_mENG and $KFHL$. Clearly the monopolistic owner gains more in profits (these two areas taken together) than it sacrifices in reduced rents. But, to repeat, the individual or group is not able to distinguish between rent-creating and profit-creating activities. The large return can be expected to generate activity by others to garner some part of the high return, as discussed at length in Chapter 4.

Government officials are not necessarily in a better position to distinguish between rent-creating and profit-creating activities, and in any case for most purposes it seems wise to rely upon the reasoned procedural safeguard, exclusive control over only a relatively small portion of any indispensable asset in any industry. Part of the problem of regulation is to determine how small "relatively small" is. This was discussed at some length in Chapter 4 where it was argued that high concentration with the leading firm controlling as much as 50 percent of the output of some product did not seem to result in monopoly power when expansion of old firms and entry of new ones is not constrained by government. The key desideratum seems to be the extent to which firms are constrained to act independently in response to their own perceptions of changing demands, substitutes, sources of supply, potential rivals, and the like rather than finding ways to contract with each other to exclude substitutes, share markets, fix input or output prices, or to find means that will exclude potential rivals at small cost. Apparently, it is hard to accomplish profitable collusive arrangements in practice. Even natural monopolies, which face rivals only in peripheral areas, seem not to have reduced efficiency greatly. Within their own areas they contend only with the ability of their larger customers to produce at high cost for themselves and they need worry only about the problematical threat of government takeover or direct regulation. But these pressures are just what one expects in a society where many interested parties can innovate and can work to change laws and regulations.

Industrywide contracts with labor unions may sometimes provide a means toward monopoly, especially when industry demand is inelastic. When union power is the essential element in raising industry returns, one must expect any increased asset values based on labor union power in the industry to redound to the leadership and membership of the union in the form of higher wages, fringes, and dues that raise costs to every firm and prices to consumers. This may include, in addition to values based on monopoly profits, some socially desirable rents that arise because no acceptable procedure for assigning rights to jobs related to the investment individuals have made in themselves has yet been discovered.

It is important to know that efforts to change social arrangements, to change starting points, have costs. Establishing new ownership rights or regulation by other means may have benefits smaller than costs. It is possible for a firm, union, or landowner with a monopoly position to be doing more net good (depart less from an optimum) than any alternative that can be conceived, once the costs of change are counted. Better policy in such cases is to seek better choices before acting, searching more diligently where the likelihood of success is greater. Application of these concepts to rental housing may help clarify the distinctions made here and their significance (see the appendix).

Application of These Principles to Advertising

The task of this section is to evaluate the social value of advertising in a frame of reference broad enough to include all the relevant variables needed by a normative theory. The evaluation is to determine whether it contributes to efficiency (enhances aggregate factor rents) or detracts from it (increases profits). First the frame of reference.

Analysis begins with the standard assumption that each individual seeks to advance his own interest (which may include the good opinion of others), but each is assumed to have imperfect knowledge of latent wants and especially of the specific alternative ways by which both lively and latent wants may be satisfied. The individual also has imperfect knowledge of his personal abilities, and even less knowledge of the abilities of others and the opportunities and terms for cooperating with them to produce, ship, or otherwise increase the value of a good or service. All agents of production and especially labor are dispersed in space, as are the consumers of the product.

It follows that learning, establishing rights of action (property rights), and contracting are essential components of the economy. Devoting resources to learning about one's desires, abilities, and opportunities is a fundamental and unavoidable part of the economic task. So are the time, effort, and resources required to make decisions about the creation, use, and maintenance of each productive agent that may have value and the effort and resources required to establish terms for the cooperative use of resources. The efficiency of an economy is increased when the benefits, net of costs, from establishing rights to make decisions are increased and when the benefit, net of costs, of contracting is increased.

Even if each individual has full and certain knowledge of his personal tastes and abilities, ignorance about those of other people impoverishes him. Information is therefore essential if he is to realize the most from his abilities as a producer and to discover the goods and services most preferred, and their prices, as a consumer. Confining attention to the special case of advertising, it is clear that information, up to some point, increases the value of the individual's ability and other property (his rents) and the value of his income (his consumer surplus). It helps him find better work opportunities and better bargains.

Too much or too little can be devoted to information provision and information seeking. At some point the improvement in opportunity is less valuable than what the resources devoted to acquiring the last bits of information would have produced had they been directed in other ways. Since information is also the output of people and their equipment, the total rents of individuals, information providers, and information seekers taken together is reduced if either too much or too little information is provided.

This presents an awkward problem of measurement. Advertising that lowers sales expense, that increases the rate of turnover, and that speeds the introduction of new products will often more than pay for itself in increased efficiency for the firms and will lower prices to consumers, as already pointed out in earlier chapters. But it also provides difficult to calculate savings in shopping time and gains in a better range of choices made available to consumers. The consumers' incomes go further, buying for the same amount of money plus search costs a greater value, but the increase in efficiency (consumer surplus, or "household rents") is not counted. Hence the gains to advertising are understated. It is probable that consumers often benefit when prices are higher because of advertising costs because for that reason they discover opportunities and shop more economically.

Substantial social gains are made because each individual and firm wisely devotes some proportion of its resources to experimentation and discovery, although only part of it is expected to have favorable results. More is allocated to experimentation and discovery when the value of additional expected favorable results outweighs the additional costs. This responds to the strong interest individuals have in novelty. Although basic wants may remain unchanged, they are satisfied in different ways and with different goods in different cultures. A common characteristic across cultures is a fascination with these differences, and, for many individuals, a strong desire to try some of them. Novelty in everyday things such as food, clothing, adornment, and art seems most sought after, but virtually nothing is exempt. This increases variety and exacerbates the inescapable problem of choice. Novelty and variety are, therefore, sought by many individuals for their own sakes and at some cost. An economy directed to the satisfaction of individual wants as the individual sees them will provide both well-known products and novelty. It will also provide information and guidelines helpful to individuals who want novelty but wish to avoid unfavorable surprises.

Critics of advertising may concede the desire for novelty, the geographical dispersion of resources, personnel, and consumers that make information an essential cost, but hold fast to the notion that information about products although necessarily incomplete can and should be unbiased. Decisions are made in conditions of uncertainty, but the cards are not to be stacked, at least not by commercially motivated enterprises. This may be the root issue of the whole controversy about advertising: the legitimacy of persuasive advertising by commercially motivated enterprises.

Are Commercially Motivated Efforts to Change Tastes Legitimate?
Critics of advertising might agree with an efficiency argument for advertising but still object to the implied premise that consumers learn well enough to be able to perceive their own best interest in a commercial environment. Wealthy businesspeople are thought to hire clever professionals, writers and artists, to mould preferences (tastes) to fit the type of products it is convenient for them to produce. The consumer instead of being sovereign is a puppet. The producer instead of winning a reward by serving the true or better needs of the population wrings a tribute from the gullible public by warping its scale of values so as to induce worship of a calf made of fool's gold. "True" satisfaction cannot be achieved by responding to the misperception of consumers, it is said.

In a sense, the objection has to do with a basic view of people— whether the ordinary person needs a preceptor or not, and, if so, who is the legitimate preceptor. For some, the first question has only one possible answer: each person is a creature of his social environment, and the environment is determined by whatever group has power. It is only a matter of which set of preceptors will win. Something like this seems to be the historical norm. Kings, dictators, or political parties claim legitimate authority and seek to impose their values using all the instruments of the civil state and a state religion besides. With the separation of church and state, in some nations, the church became the ostensible repositor of moral teaching, of "correct" value judgments. The state no less than the economy, in principle at least, only served the moral order as perceived by ecclesiastical authority. In modern states that recognize a multiplicity of religions, including the beliefs of atheists and humanists, the national state again assumes ascendancy as preceptor, especially where it is dominated by a totalitarian party that has made all other parties illegal and tamed religious authority. The intellectual case contesting government regulation of advertising on the ground that it is a source of power over "tastes" and beliefs cannot rationally neglect this fundamental root of disagreement—the questioned legitimacy of commercial, or material, appeals that affect or seem to affect the value systems of individuals composing the society. The legitimacy of using the power of government officials to attempt to control tastes is also an issue.

It is time to drop the assumption that consumers know what they want and go back to our original position that although there may be some stable basic wants felt by consumers, all of us must learn about them, find ways to satisfy them, and put them in some sort of order of priorities. We have imperfect knowledge of our wants and how to satisfy them. Is it desirable that self-interested merchants be among our instructors? If it is, may they produce whatever will sell and advertise it as they wish? Could consumers (children and the insane excepted) choose wisely even if advertising were in fact honest and informative? Would they if they could? Truthful, nondeceptive advertising in the opinion of many opponents of advertising will not avoid the harmful effects of cigarettes, abortions, handguns, or trail bikes— to name only a few of the goods much desired by some but considered by others to be socially harmful—and, therefore, if not to be banned outright, at least to be forbidden the opportunity to advertise, no matter how truthfully and completely. Mistrust of the reasonableness of other people and a desire to impose wiser choices on them "for their own good" perhaps lies at the bottom of some complaints directed against advertising. But the costs as well as the benefits of alternatives need to be evaluated.[8]

The question comes down to: Who should be permitted to deter-

---

[8]See two excellent studies by Sam Peltzman: "The Effects of Automobile Safety Regulation," *Journal of Political Economy*, vol. 83 (August 1976), pp. 677–726; and *Regulation of Pharmaceutical Innovation*.

mine the legally sanctioned range of choices open to individuals? and Who may influence their search among the available choices? Economic theory does not deal with these problems directly. Nevertheless, the economic approach is highly relevant because it avoids a common-sense pitfall that simply assumes a close correspondence between professed or implied motivation and consequences.

Irrelevance of the Advertiser's Motivation. Adam Smith's famous insight, as every literate person should know, is that it is not out of sympathy that the baker provides us with bread but out of regard for his own self-interest. He may well have pride in his work, and a desire to serve others, but the objective test of the value of his service, and his source of untroubled pride, lies in the consumer's choice of his product over that of others. Thus he seeks the consumer's favor out of self-interest, but is led to serve it well. In the larger frame, the baker could do other things of value to others, but in choosing to be a baker he satisfies both himself and his customers more fully than he could by any alternative known to him. Smith says that he is led to serve others although it is no part of his intention. But if it is not, *it is only a failure of the baker's insight.* Understanding Smith's point, the baker would also know that he was serving optimally the discoverable wants of consumers as they express their wants. Nevertheless, from a scientific point of view, the presence or absence of the baker's insight is beside the point. He does so serve, and any testable hypothesis stands unaltered without his insight.

An even more important insight found in Adam Smith's work is that an economic system using markets to coordinate the activities of millions of inhabitants is in fact effectively organized to serve their needs. This insight obliterates the need for moral leaders to divide and lead the various tribal, national, racial, or sex categories of humanity against each other, and it allows (without requiring) the treatment of persons as individuals not conscripts. For obvious reasons, most of the leaders of politically active groups either do not understand this idea, are willfully blind to it, or believe it to be inappropriate to today's world. Unfortunately, the majority of the world's intellectuals support these leaders. Still, in a system of rivalry without direct regulation, Adam Smith's celebrated but scorned conception that self-interested sellers will be led by an invisible hand to benefit the public interest although it is *no part of their intention* may approximately hold true. Net benefits, even if small, may be larger than those realizable under alternative arrangements.

Direct Public Regulation—A Malevolent Invisible Hand? The Founding Fathers, whose Declaration of Independence appeared in the same year as Adam Smith's *Wealth of Nations*, seemed to be on guard against a malevolent invisible hand when they drew up the U.S. Constitution in 1787. Their care in limiting government power and dividing that deemed helpful among the federal government, the states, and the people; and that allocated to the federal government and the states among legislative, executive, and judicial branches; and the initial amendments to provide a secure basis for a Fourth Estate separate from government presupposes an inverted form of Adam Smith's insight. Too often individuals, when acting in official capacity as agents with government powers to advance the public interest, are seemingly led by an invisible hand to act against the public welfare, although it is no part of *their* intention and despite well-intentioned toil to give substance to their solemn oaths.

The issue comes down to a contest between a libertarian and a paternalistic conception of government. Libertarians are willing to accept the patterns of behavior and purchases that result from uncensored information and persuasion and the free introduction of products and services. Paternalists are willing to use the power of government to impose some limits on information, persuasion, organizations, products, and services. The extreme form of paternalism is totalitarianism, where government attempts to produce or control all goods and services and all messages on all information media.

Can Regulation of Advertising Change Tastes Significantly? Most real systems display some degree of paternalism, which in Western nations may with some degree of accuracy be termed democratic elitism. It is democratic both in the Western procedural sense of coming out of a process that gives some influence to the views of each of many divergent groups and in the Communist sense of reflecting a position approved by spokespeople for a presumed majority of the people. It is elitist in the sense of imposing majority values on many who do not accept them, and not merely by trying to persuade but also by criminalizing the goods, services, or acts objected to. It seems logical enough to extend paternalism into borderline areas by subjecting certain products and services to special taxes, or, as is relevant here, by limiting or banning the advertising of products thought by opinion-setters to inculcate or intensify socially undesirable tastes when for some reason or another they are not prepared to ban the product outright.

Banning the product would seem to be the more effective way to diminish the use of, and in time the desire for, the questionable goods and services. It raises the cost to users far more than restrictive advertising, more even than prohibitive taxation, because of the penalties for being caught. The increased cost of lessened blandishments and limitations on knowledge of availability, quality, and price because of limited or banned advertising appear minor in comparison. Yet these far stronger measures do not suffice to engineer tastes to the satisfaction of former or present controllers. Perhaps nothing illustrates this better than the American experience with alcoholic beverages. The Eighteenth Amendment to the Constitution of the United States was to improve the quality of lives and homes by prohibiting the manufacture, sale, and possession of alcoholic beverages. The Amendment cleared Congress on December 18, 1917, and secured ratification by the thirty-sixth state on January 29, 1919. It was passed in large part in response to pressures from the Woman's Christian Temperance Union and various Protestant denominations. At the time, having successfully mobilized to win "the war to end wars," the door seemed open to permanent improvement by changing laws and regulations. In less than five years, opium was placed under regulation, quotas were placed on immigration, and voting was liberalized by the extension of the suffrage to women. The Volstead Act, designed to enforce the Eighteenth Amendment, was passed by Congress over President Wilson's veto in October 1919.

Social Costs of Efforts to Change Tastes. The amendment was in effect from January 29, 1920, until its repeal became effective December 5, 1933. It had some impact on consumption and its effects, but less than might be expected.[9] The criminalized industry did not lack for customers. Al Capone is reported to have said that he was never able to meet the demand that came from all classes of people, including the best. Apparently neither severe constraints, of which the elimination of advertising was among the least, nor vigorous counteradvertising by "moral leaders" and many politicians changed tastes much or effectively denied access to the means of satisfaction. What it did do was to criminalize a large part of the electorate, provide a rich source of income to criminal elements in society who already knew how to operate banned enterprises (notably prostitution, gambling, and high interest loans), drastically lower the quality and reliability of the banned products, eliminate safe means of redress for consumers or heirs poisoned by defective items, and substantially raise the product's price. It also provided wealth for government officials willing to be bribed, or vulnerable to blackmail, and it tended to attract people of this type to political and appointive office.

---

[9]Irving Fisher, *A Prohibition at Its Worst* (New York: Macmillan, 1926). Fisher, the preeminent American economist at the time and a strong prohibitionist, presents tables that show a substantial recovery of alcohol consumption even by the time he wrote.

The criminalization of the nonprescription narcotic industry that began in the 1920s has a similar history. Its sorry record has not yet resulted in repeal. Abortion is no longer banned, and restrictions on pornography are disappearing, but faith in prohibition (criminalization) remains. If consumers or citizens are not dissuaded by mandated truthful and relevant advertising, public interest counteradvertising, and education, many opinion leaders would criminalize the production and sale of such things as flammable fabrics, cyclamates, and automobiles with low gasoline mileage. The same approach is taken toward low wages, market prices for natural gas, disproportionate numbers of employees of each race or sex, and insufficient ethnic diversity in public schools. Enforcement difficulties reveal the ineffectiveness of paternalistic pressures to change tastes when they go beyond information and persuasion to direct control of the product or service itself. With the desires remaining virtually untouched, the attempts to satisfy them become less satisfactory—and more destructive, costly, and harmful to the social fabric.

The widespread demand and supply of recreational drugs offers an instance where advertising and promotion can have no present influence because mere possession of the product is itself a crime. One may wonder where the balance of consumer protection would lie if instead of the present structure of untrademarked, unadvertised, illegal production and sale of recreational drugs we had a system of legal, advertised, and trademarked production and sale of the same goods. The latter has some important points in its favor. Quality, especially uniformity and purity, would certainly be higher in the legal industry. Private competition for sales and enforceable producer and merchandiser liability would see to that. Fewer deaths would result from unintended overdose due to lack of knowledge, uncertain potency, and purity. Prices would surely be lower because risks to the suppliers would be drastically reduced. Drug traffic could not be used as a source of income for criminals, for domestic or foreign-based political revolutionaries, or for similarly illegal groups.

Against this, the lower prices and improved quality could be expected to increase the number of users. It is not possible to say whether decriminalization would increase the number of addicts. In nations such as Turkey, where use of opium and its derivatives is long standing, the social problem is said to be moderate, perhaps less troublesome than Western experience with alcohol now that alcohol is legal, trademarked, advertised, and produced by relatively few large producers and many small ones, all of whom are financially and legally liable.

Today there is perhaps more evidence that government policies

116

adopted in the belief that they would improve matters have instead done ill than there is evidence that private decision making has had overall untoward effects. Too many recently instituted programs founded and funded with good intentions and sacrifice—sometimes extorted by finely tuned feelings of intergenerational guilt—are rightly perceived to have gone astray. Yet government agencies, responding to many diverse pressures in and out of government, continue to strain against the stretched and fraying social and constitutional bounds that still limit their power.

It is natural for government officials to stretch their power and their status relative to whatever benchmark groups can be found. Advertising by self-interested businesspeople offers an attractive opportunity. All agree that business must pay significant attention to the "bottom line" if it is to survive, so successful businesses of necessity have been successfully managed to advance the interests of their owners and managers. Regulation of commercial speech, advertising, is a small matter to the electorate and one where the good intentions of government may contrast favorably in the electorate's view to the self-interested intentions of the advertiser. Yet the regulation of advertising along the lines suggested by Comanor and Wilson provides a strategically placed fulcrum for a long lever that can introduce detailed supervision into sectors of the economy that now serve the public well, better than they can if regulated.

Why Regulation Tends to Become More Intensive and Costly. The power of government inclines the officials who would improve the quality of life to move to ever more intensive efforts. It begins with a moral judgment. If voluntary restriction is deemed inefficient, it proceeds to infringement on the right of offenders to persuade (to advertise their products or views), and it goes on to discourage use with special taxes. When that does not suffice, officials argue that they are "forced" to place production under tight governmental controls. Next, the production and sale may be prohibited outright. The penultimate step is to make possession or participation as a consumer a crime. Finally, warrantless searches are authorized, together with immediate confiscation and perhaps prompt destruction of any illegal property discovered. As we have seen, alcoholic beverages and some drugs have run the full gamut and returned part of the way. Cigarettes are in the third stage, and gasoline the fourth, except that advertising is only under scrutiny by various legislative and administrative committees. But the brute fact is that the full weight of authority does not effectively change tastes very much. Instead it offers a symbol of protest and a source of income and wealth to criminal organizations.

117

A more optimistic view of humanity that relies on education to deal with risks and inflated appeals rather than laws intended to remove all hazards and protect against all disappointments caused by credulity may also be the more hard-headed and fruitful view. In that case, one does not pass beyond the first stage, the moral judgment. False or inflated claims made by advertising are countered by the skepticism of the potential customer, counteradvertising by rivals; ratings by agencies that provide evidence of their impartiality; consumer magazines that must hold their readers by doing a good job; protection in the courts, where damages are suffered because of the fault of the producer; and, perhaps, government certification of the accuracy of claims made for products voluntarily submitted to it.

Private Monopoly Power from Advertising Reviewed: Limits on Private Power

Perspective on government power to persuade and dissuade should reassure those who fear the influence of private enterprises. Each must contend with the counteradvertising of rivals, plus the presumably less biased revelations of a free press; a multifaceted legislative and administrative set of inquisitors at the federal, state, and local levels; and with actual and potential court suits, to say nothing of the appearance of new rivals from at home and abroad if it seems to be making profits above the average.

Already emphasized, but still almost universally overlooked, is the most striking fact to come out of studies of U.S. industry: observed profit rates and observed elasticities of demand are incompatible with each of the popular hypotheses that links scarcity of sellers and relatively large size of the leading sellers to monopoly prices. This incompatibility is obscured by correlations of profit with concentration that, although statistically significant, indicate profits far lower than predicted by the theories of oligopoly referred to when determining the sign to be expected for the relationship.[10] It is obscured even more completely by purely formal statements of plausible relationships that

---

[10]See, for example, Strickland and Weiss, "Advertising, Concentration, and Price-Cost Margins." This interesting analysis of 408 industries treats 102 of the consumer goods separately from the others. The price-cost margin increases slightly less than one-tenth of one percent with each percentage increase in concentration. A concentration ratio of 100 will not produce the margins profit maximization associated with low elasticities. Interestingly, this study concludes that although "advertising leads to greater concentration" (p. 1111), the results suggest "that the product differentiation barrier to entry is not very great" (p. 1120). However, the combination of plant scale and concentration is positively and significantly related to price-cost margins.

are not compared to any body of data, but which, nevertheless, are published in major journals.[11]

In fact, the profit margins in both concentrated and unconcentrated industry are close to the cost of capital.[12] Either the firms thought to have market power are not interested in high profits or they do not have significant monopoly power even when concentration ratios are high. Either way, consumer interests and the public interest are well-served.

Firms do not have the power to act differently because of constraints including those listed at the beginning of this section. The result of these constraints is to force a large element of independence into firms' strategies, making them sensitive to the potential that other firms have to expand and to the potential loss of customers to other firms producing similar and not so similar products. Thus the demand curve as perceived by the firm, the one relevant to its decisions, is much more elastic than the demand curve for its industry, and the more profitable markup is far less than the one indicated by the low elasticities of industry demand curves. In addition, the desire of the larger firms to set higher markups is disciplined by the willingness of smaller firms to accept smaller markups, and their actual and potential ability to expand. This explanation is at least consistent with available data.

If one accepts this explanation for the paradox of coexisting high concentration and competitive markups, most activities that have restrictionist overtones—such as the careful protection of trademarks, establishment of a favorable public image by public relations and advertising, and other devices employed to enhance the value of a firm's resources—take on the character of rent-creation, not profit-making, as the terms are defined here. Restrictions would be monopolistic only if individual decision makers were to have control that extends so widely as to affect the total supply of an industry.

Bases for Effective Power. So far, the facts strongly suggest the absence of significant monopoly power even in industries characterized by high concentration. On the other hand significant monopoly pricing has been discovered in two professions (optometry and pharmacy) and in an industry where concentration is very low and the largest firms are small (trucks). Evidently, one must look for some very widespread contract or agreement that performs two functions—restriction of entry and limited competition among the enterprises already operat-

---

[11]For example, Bergson, "On Monopoly Welfare Losses."
[12]See Alberts, "Why Are Welfare Losses from Monopoly Small?"

ing. These exist most effectively when there is some kind of formal contract that is legally enforceable.

Two types of contracts of this sort are the most common. One is a legal requirement that an operator have an official license or franchise with the total number granted and controlled by an interested source. This type is especially effective when continued rights to work in the licensed activity are conditional on anticompetitive practices, such as avoidance of advertising and adherence to set or minimum fee schedules. The second type is contracts where all producers at some broad stage of production agree with a third party with control over an essential input, such as labor, to a monopolistic factor price. In that case, the sellers closer to the consumer have higher costs of production and simply cannot find a way to expand output closer to the optimal level. The third party can restrict the supply of the essential input, and therefore industry output, enough to provide a high income for its members and higher returns for the other parties to the contract. From time to time the contract will be rewritten to bring it up to date and to reallocate the gains. This type of agreement is not possible without tacit government support for the position of the third party. Without such support rivals would find a way to produce the good or service at lower cost.

The Key Issue

The key clue to the difference between rights that increase efficiency, or rents, and those that increase profits, as defined here, lies in the extent to which control of all of a necessary resource is dispersed. *Any* input may be a power-giving resource. This includes each approval required from each government agency if a project is to proceed.

Studies of enterprise monopoly show nearly competitive behavior, even when industries display high concentration ratios, provided that they have not been "rationalized" by government. When they are, low concentration is no barrier to monopoly power.

More research is necessary to estimate how much concentration of "ownership" (ability to exclude) by any decision-making unit is consistent with efficiency. I offer the hypothesis that 50 percent is not too much when rivalry is unconstrained. Presently, some product lines are controlled almost 100 percent by a single decision-making unit. Most such units are either public utilities, professions, or labor unions. In more instances there is some competition, for example, from foreign sources. Tests should be possible. The possibility that even 100 percent of the market will be found efficient in some cases of "natural monopoly" or where potential competition exists is not excluded.

120

Government regulation of advertising carries potential monopoly power in many markets. The following propositions are advanced for use in formulating policies regarding such regulation.

- Evidence strongly indicates that government limitations on advertising that go beyond the prevention of untruthful statements are destructive of values to consumers.
- Government requirements that the producer of a good or service be clearly identified with a trademark and/or a brand name increases the liability of the producer for unsatisfactory products and increases values for consumers.
- There is reason to believe that the self-interested statements of the producer of a good or service give greater benefits to consumers than do other alternatives, as long as private evaluations of the products can be published and the opportunity to sue for damages is protected.
- There is little reason to believe that there is now too much advertising.

(1) *Government regulation reduces total values (aggregate factor rents).* The studies that support the first proposition will not be reviewed here, since a review would only repeat the findings for eyeglasses, prescription drugs, and toys summarized in Chapter 3. In all cases, advertising appears on the side of competition and regulation of advertising on the side of monopoly. Regulations to standardize the quality and strength of drugs, and make them known on the label, adds value to the product, although one may question how far it goes beyond the information desired by buyers that a self-interested competitive firm would find it in its interest to include. But regulation in the sense of the compulsory elimination of some products is not supported. Those favoring regulation focus attention on the potential lives saved and neglect the number of lives actually lost because of delays or permanent (legal) unavailability and the higher cost of approved substances.

(2) *Trademarks and brand names increase total values (factor rents).* Investigations show advertising to be in some degree an investment. This gives firms an incentive to produce recognizable products of uniform quality. Disappointed customers who do not find what they expected, or later become disgruntled, cut the value of the investment. The loss of value is more pronounced the more readily available are competing products. Thus mechanisms exist that provide powerful incentives for firms to produce good products and seek better values—to make them known in ways that do not create disappointment and are attractive, that cater to the desire for pleasant discovery, while at the same time motivating consumers to take care, husbanding

resources and dividing them intelligently between the tried and true and the exploratory. All this occurs in the absence of government action to regulate the quality, safety, or effectiveness of products or the truthfulness, adequacy, or appeal of selling efforts.

No government is, or has been, content to leave it at that. At the very least laws require identification of manufacturers so that liability for damages can be assigned when damage results from faulty products. That firms take the mark of liability, the trademark, and attempt to convert it into a mark of quality only attests to the ingenuity and self-interest of the managers of firms and the effectiveness of the requirement. With branding comes the possibility of guarantees and other assumed liabilities that express producer confidence in the product.

The guarantee itself may, however, be deceptive. Moreover, trademarks can be imitated so that quality built up by one company is "stolen" by another with a similar brand name or mark. The legal requirement of branding therefore requires exclusive use by a manufacturer and sellers of a given brand, and, for that reason legal protection of the trademark is an important part of the assignment of rights whether the brand comes to be an asset or a liability. The costs of requiring and protecting brand names and trademarks are borne directly or indirectly by the generality of the population in their roles as consumers or taxpayers. The net effect may, in principle, be either beneficial or costly to buyers, but its beneficial effect seems to prevail by a wide margin. Consider cases where it seems to confer monopoly power. Sometimes a brand name comes to be applied to a whole category of goods. Thus Frigidaire came to designate any electric refrigerator, and in Russia Studebaker simply meant very good. Does possession of such a name confer an undesirable amount of market power? Perhaps not. Ownership of such a name has a double-edged quality because a rival that can demonstrate equality or superiority to a well-known product can make rapid inroads. The virtual universality of branding in Western countries suggests it has substantial positive value. Protection of private assets based on branding is a logical counterpart of insisting on the liabilities they impose.

(3) *Partial information provided by interested sellers is beneficial to consumers.* At this point the earlier discussion of the relative merit of partial and impartial information from the point of view of the consumer is recalled. It is appropriate to note that considerable protection is available to worried consumers who suspect that they may be in need of a costly, technical, and rarely used good or service beyond their personal abilities to evaluate. In such instances there is a market for experts, intermediate enterprisers who evaluate the goods and ser-

vices of primary producers and sell their knowledge to final consumers. Thus, while the consumer cannot engage significantly in direct exploratory behavior, it is often possible to make a choice among specialist agents whose success or failure builds a reputation in their community. Often their knowledge is of particular value only in the locality, and their reputation is their principal asset. This is helpful in the purchase of medical care, legal services, insurance, and financial planning. In retail trade, department and variety stores, especially those long in a community, have an interest in careful selection and satisfied customers.

This is not to say that the consumer is relying on disinterested "professional" advice. While professionalism exists, it is more often a form of self-interest rather than of altruism. At one time it was believed that one could count on disinterested service from practitioners of recognized professions, especially medicine, law, academia, and the ministry, simply because of the moral or official character of the practitioners. Now they are often viewed as special subsets of skilled employees or business persons whose actions are explicable by reference to their self-interest. Still, each practitioner of these professions does earn largely on the basis of his or her reputation in the community, and each deals with many clients who are willing, often eager, to tell friends and neighbors about the satisfaction they received or did not receive. Law offices, medical clinics, universities, and churches have, therefore, strong reasons to screen and instruct new professionals joining their enterprises in order to serve their clients well.

Consumers are better served by positive devices to make truthful statements by less well-known suppliers creditable, rather than by seeking control or surveillance over all advertising. The monopoly power exercised by means of a professional "ethical" prohibition of advertising for eyeglasses and drugs, cited earlier, shows how such power can make services of no better quality more costly to consumers. In these cases, professionals earn monopoly profits and rents are smaller than they would otherwise be. Increasing competition among professionals by encouraging rather than restricting advertising seems more likely to produce results beneficial to consumers—increasing rents and reducing profits, as the terms are defined here. Government restrictions can be expected to have similar effects.

(4) *Too many resources are not devoted to advertising.* Critics of advertising rarely argue that advertising should be eliminated, and they may not be surprised that private arrangements to inhibit advertising are associated with higher prices to consumers. But the argument is made that consumers are subjected to uneconomically large amounts of advertising because it is produced jointly with entertainment, espe-

cially on radio and TV. The positive value of the entertainment is partially offset by the negative value of the commercials, yielding a joint return whose average value is about equal to the marginal cost of viewing and/or listening to the station. This argument seems mistaken.

The difficulty with this argument lies in the mass production characteristics of these media and competition among them. In spite of their efforts, each station inevitably produces a mix of types of entertainment, news, and advertising that fails to meet the exact preferences and needs of every individual viewer.

The consumer pays the following: purchase of access, say a TV; purchase of the necessary power, et cetera; and expenditure of time viewing. The consumer gets some entertainment he wants and some he feels was a waste of time, or worse, plus some advertising of value to him and some of no value. The consumer watches until the probable gain from spending more time is equal to the alternative value of his time. Some messages carry very little information. Yet, as Philip Nelson has shown, the simple fact that a firm is willing to spend money to bring a product to the attention of those who already know they want a product of that type is of value to the consumer.[13]

To repeat, the consumer pays for his radio and TV in money and in kind (his viewing time) to receive valuable entertainment and advertising. The advertiser pays enough to cover the advertising and at least part of the entertainment. On commercial TV and radio the advertiser pays all of both, including public service programs, which generally have a smaller audience, making commercial sponsorship of the public service programs (and the time slots that follow them) less valuable to advertisers. There are gains to many viewers from public service programs that may not be useful to advertisers. The owners of the media, radio and TV in our example, compete to find the mix of qualities and timing of entertainment, advertising, and public service programs that will magnify their incomes. But too little time is likely to be devoted to advertising and to entertainment because government authorities, which may or may not be responsive to consumer interests, insist on a larger than optimal number of public service programs.

Competition among the owners of the media puts an edge on the impulse to make the advertisers pay as much as possible. The advertisers will pay more according to the size and receptivity of the audience the media can command. Since viewers have many uses of their time, including shopping, garage sales, coffee klatches, and the like, where

---

[13]Philip Nelson, "Advertising as Information," *Journal of Political Economy,* vol. 82 (July/August 1974), pp. 729–54.

knowledge about goods and services is exchanged, the size of the audience and the numbers who will be interested in the commercials are determined ultimately by the insight and skill of putting together attractive combinations of entertainment, news, public service programs, and advertisements. If the station managers succeed, at the margin each of these will tend to have the same value to the viewers, the station owners, and the advertisers. If too much advertising is scheduled, or if it is too offensive or irrelevant, viewers are lost to other channels, other media, or to tennis, golf, or other activities, and less can be charged for air time. The same holds for other aspects of programming.

Advertising seems excessive because it is necessarily a mass production industry. The reasons for mass advertising are the lack of knowledge on the part of businesspeople about who their customers may be and lack of knowledge by individuals about just what preferences they can satisfy, just what different products will do, where they may be obtained, and on what terms and at what price. Despite their best efforts, businesspeople will find it cheaper to place their messages before many more people who are not interested than who are. This is equally true of charities that find it cheaper to send solicitations, with the added cost of including in the original and the redundant copies a note begging pardon if you receive "more than one" (maybe five) pleas, rather than undertaking the cost of comparing lists and sending only one. Similarly it is inevitable that every consumer will regret much time taken viewing part or all of the messages that turn out to be of no interest to him. He will have similar feelings about the other programming. Nevertheless, the most efficient choices among all presently known possibilities involve the mass production of messages. Disciplined, intelligent endeavor simply has not, thus far, been able to discover a less expensive way to communicate.

So far this chapter has argued that an economic theory useful for the examination of advertising must take into account the dispersion of individuals in their dual capacities of productive resource owners and ultimate consumers and the fact that the range of opportunities open to each one far exceeds those that can be investigated by personal experience. Thus informational problems are unavoidable in individual capacities as consumers and as producers. Each individual can be expected to seek his own fulfillment, and the information he generates for others must be assumed to be biased in his favor. Yet there are restraints that tend to make information truthful even in the absence of government action and additional constraints when the products are legal and can be advertised. The banning or restrictive regulation of advertising seems, on the record, to be harmful.

Advertising and Rent-Creation

The subject matter of this chapter has sometimes moved away from the central concern of this study as a whole because no way could be found to connect advertising to monopoly profit. Instead, advertising enhances rents, and therefore efficiency.

There is no point in advertising something one does not own and less point in advertising something no one wants. Advertising can be effective only if it enhances the value of a product to someone. Advertising a product contributes to the liability of the advertiser should the product fail or otherwise damage the buyer. It ties the seller to the product in a way that makes him much more vulnerable than the fly-by-night who is hard to find if the customer is hurt or dissatisfied. So advertising adds to consumer surplus by lowering the consumer's costs of search and increasing the degree of confidence a buyer can repose in the product as compared with available unadvertised alternatives.

Some believe that disinterested evaluation is superior to self-interested promotion. A comparison of *Consumer Reports* with Sear's catalog casts doubts on this position from the standpoints of effectiveness in informing the customer, disciplining the competition, and assuming responsibility for what is said. "Disinterested information," especially if it displaces and excludes self-interested advertising, carries far greater threat of monopoly than any one firm could bring to bear, even in a single firm monopoly. Such a firm still faces potential competition from new entrants. Information is one of the inputs of every firm. Control of information confers monopoly power on the controller, whose stated opinion becomes a vitally needed complement in the protective process.

The power of advertising is limited. It cannot extinguish the demand for a class of products—witness the current campaign against recreational drugs and the campaign against alcohol in the 1920s. Nor can it create more than a momentary demand for something that is not wanted. This is not to say that it is without influence. Its influence is related to the nature of the product, the state of competition, and the nature of the demand by consumers. If the consumer has a desire for novelty, if the firms are actively introducing modified products, if new firms have a product for which they want to get substantial acceptance before others can copy it, if the use of the product is not obvious, or if it is used infrequently by any one buyer, then advertising expenditures valuable to consumers will be high.

Successful products will have higher volume, higher turnover, and higher profits at comparable or lower prices than their rivals.

While advertising plays a role in this, it is not "the cause," nor is the higher return of the more successful rivals a monopoly profit. It is a rent to management, much, but not all of which, will get to those who wove the web of decisions that had the exceptional result. The value of the enterprise is higher because it used its resources more efficiently, not because it restricted opportunity for others by denying them access to, or raised the cost of, some whole category of resource needed to compete with them. If the larger firms enjoy scale economies, it is because they grew enough to benefit from them. Their existence does not deny a smaller rival the opportunity to grow. Instead it demonstrates the possibility of achieving scale economies, something that could only have been conjectured before, and, in the absence of the demonstration, attempted only with greater risk.

It is important that firms be made liable for what they sell, which is to say that they provide adequate information about what their products and services can do and what hazards are involved in foreseeable misuses. Very likely, consumers are misled more seriously by door-to-door salespersons who are not connected with a reliable firm and cannot be located if things go wrong. Something needs to be done, if it does not cost too much, to make these sellers subject to liability for fraud and damages. But door-to-door salespersons backed by well-known firms that advertise are a lesser threat and a greater opportunity for the customer precisely because they are heavy advertisers and for that reason well-known and desirous of selling in such a way as to enhance their reputation, which for them is a valuable asset. One could say they wish to enhance their profits, but while this is true from their point of view, what they are doing from a social point of view is enhancing the value to consumers of their management organization, or the insight and productivity of some key person in the organization; in a word, its factor rents.

APPENDIX

Rentals: An Example

Two illustrations clarify the distinction between factor rents (as the term is used here) that improve efficiency and factor profits that diminish it. The illustrations relate to a durable good (housing) and a natural resource (fish). To simplify the argument, it is assumed that there is no cost of assigning rights.

Imagine an isolated town in which there are 2,500 apartments owned either by 100 private owners or collectively through a public housing corporation. Suppose further that the rent presently charged covers maintenance and interest, and results in a 5 percent vacancy rate (125 apartments). The vacancy rate enhances the value of the apartments by allowing individual households to shift quickly to other quarters as their housing requirements change. Suppose that this equilibrium is disturbed by an edict that makes the payment or receipt of any rental illegal, and also forbids the occupancy of more than one unit by any one household. The immediate consequence of this edict would be to remove the incentive and, before long, the ability of the owners, public or private, to make repairs.

Even if property taxes are also abolished, the usefulness of the occupied apartments would soon be impaired unless it is in the tenants' interest fully to maintain the units at their own expense. This is not likely as long as the 125 vacant apartments are available in good repair and tenants have the option of moving into them. Part of the stock of apartments will thus deteriorate and be converted into a throwaway good. The remaining 2,375 units will also deteriorate unless the individuals who happen to occupy them get as much satisfaction from their housing as before, and can maintain the units as economically as the former owner-managers. Neither is to be expected. It will be harder to move from one size and quality of apartment to another as size of household and desires change because of the absence of vacant units. Thus people will put up with less suitable housing. Getting less from it, they will be less willing to spend money to maintain it. Maintenance and repair expenses will also cost more because the individual tenants, not being specialists in this line of work, will be less well informed and less able to manage repair and maintenance. Consequently, the real cost of an apartment to a tenant will rise, in part because the utility derivable from the housing is reduced, and in part because the cost to the tenants of maintaining a given quantity and quality is increased.

To summarize, the abolition of rental payments reduces to zero the value of the stock of housing to its owners, while raising the real cost of housing to the tenants by a combination of quality deterioration, reduced availability, and increased repair and maintenance costs. All this is avoided if owners are allowed to maximize their factor rents. Competition among a number of apartment owners or appropriate decisions of a rent-maximizing housing authority would maximize the value of the holdings and simultaneously provide a more valuable, lower-cost service to tenants.

Now consider the situation where factor profits, not factor rents, are maximized. Suppose that the 100 owners, or the government, act as a monopolist. By taking 125 apartments (5 percent) off the market, they find that they can raise the annual rental by 5 percent (or, alternatively, when they raise the rents 5 percent they find they can keep only 2,375 units rented). Thus the annual income from the smaller number of apartments remains as high as before, and the owners do not have the expense of repairing, paying taxes on, and managing the ones closed down.

This higher return, over and above that needed to maintain the larger number of apartments in a constant state of repair, is a return to monopolistic privilege, a factor profit. Whether the profit arises from the initial reduction of supply or from charging an excessive price, it is based on the ability to reduce the *total* supply of apartments. This ability is a monopoly privilege that is separate from the ownership of apartments. It exists when a single decision-making unit is allowed to have control over too many resources of the *same type* in the *same market*. Thus ownership has no monopoly value unless it can prevent others from building new apartments for rent. Its value is also limited by such factors as the availability of houses for purchase.

The total return to the monopolist, the rental, has come to include both factor rents and factor profits. This return on the 2,375 units is greater than the rent alone for the 2,500 apartments. If this were not so, the monopoly privilege would be worthless. Factor rent falls, but not by as much as factor profit increases. Monopolization reduces efficiency, although not as much as would a legislated reduction of rentals to zero, because the monopolist is more efficient than the tenants at organizing repair and maintenance.

The distinction between rents and profits, highlighted in this example, is often obscure in practical situations. The capitalized value of the rent plus monopoly profit indicates that the apartments increase in value after the number is reduced and the rentals raised. The damage to the renters, while real, is harder to estimate. But an empirical way to separate the two is available. If it is made easy to build apartments that can be rented at the discretion of the owners and if only a limited number can be under the control of any one management, then a high rental will attract more builders who can make more in the apartment business than in any alternative activity. Any high return will be temporary because rivals are not excluded by a monopoly privilege. A short-run high return can—I think improperly—be called a monopoly profit, but it rests on foresight, or perhaps luck, not on privilege, and it serves the socially useful purpose of attracting investment and expanding assets until returns become too small to attract additional resources from other opportunities. According to this interpretation, the high rental effectively improves efficiency in the market. In a sense it is a necessary cost of discovering inefficiencies and of making adjustments that improve efficiency. It is a factor rent to entrepreneurship. It may also be thought of as ordinary profit as distinguished from monopoly profit.

Ocean fisheries provide a good example of an industry where inefficiency results from the inability or refusal to charge appropriate rents. If anyone can fish, the number of fishermen and the amount of capital devoted to fishing will expand until the earnings in the industry yield wages comparable to those earned elsewhere by people of the same ability and until the return on capital is no greater than that earned in other enterprises. No monopoly profit will be received and no rents will be paid to use the valuable resource, the fishery.

In the case of a single fishery, one of many, which produces 2 percent of the total, the price of fish will be little affected by doubling or halving the output of this fishery. What then will limit its expansion? It is limited by the declining catch per boat as the number of boats and fishermen increases. This raises the cost per fish for every boat, as illustrated by the two supply curves in Figures 5 and 6 (Chapter 5). From the standpoint of efficiency, no additional boats should fish once the value added to the total from the fishery is no more than the cost of one boat and its crew. But without factor rents to the resource itself, every boat in the fishery will have a return that is increased by the amount of its share of the rental that is not paid. Therefore, additional